More Paradoxes

Henri De Lubac

More Paradoxes

Translated by
Anne Englund Nash

IGNATIUS PRESS   SAN FRANCISCO

Title of the French original:
Autres paradoxes
© 1994 Culture et vérité, Namur

Cover calligraphy by Victoria Hoke Lane
Cover design by Roxanne Mei Lum

© 2002 Ignatius Press, San Francisco
All rights reserved
ISBN 0-89870-864-8
Library of Congress Control Number 2001095549
Printed in the United States of America ∞

Contents

Foreword	7
I Gospel	11
II Council. Collegiality. Para- and Post-Council	39
III Mysteries, Doctrine, Tradition, Faith	71
IV The Rock of Faith	115
APPENDIX: "To *Jesu Crucificado*"	131

Foreword

> In his free time in Lyons, Fumet dreamed too of creating in Paris a series, and even a publishing house, in the wake of *Temps présent*. He snatched *Paradoxes* (1946) from me, most of which dates from before the war; this was the first, I believe, of his series of "Cailloux blancs". An excellent writer and shrewd critic, Fumet was the least commercial of men. It took no time at all, of course, for his house to go bankrupt. After various transfers, my little book ended by falling into the basement of Éditions du Seuil, from which it had some trouble getting out. Yet there was a subsequent *Nouveaux Paradoxes*, then an edition that joined these two works into a single, somewhat augmented volume.[1]

That is the end of the rather eventful history of *Paradoxes*. In 1989, in his office on rue de Grenelle, Cardinal Henri de Lubac put in my hands a packet of typed pages, organized by subject, with the words "Do what you want with it." It was the manuscript we are now publishing. Then, among the papers left in his room at the Little Sisters of the Poor on avenue de Breteuil, I

[1] Henri de Lubac, *At the Service of the Church: Henri de Lubac Reflects on the Circumstances that Occasioned His Writings*, trans. Anne Elizabeth Englund (San Francisco: Ignatius Press, Communio Books, 1993), p. 41.

found a packet of mostly manuscript notes, already divided into four parts and a bit more numerous than those in the first packet Father de Lubac had delivered: it was a draft of this manuscript. It bore the title *Other Paradoxes*; similarly, the first two parts were entitled, respectively, "Gospel" and "Council. Collegiality. Para- and Post-Council". We have kept these titles; those of the last two parts were supplied by the publisher.

These *Paradoxes* were written between the end of the Council (1965) and at the earliest 1983, the latest attested date.[2] On the other hand, some of the excesses referred to (Bultmannian criticism of the Gospels, praise of secularization, liturgical and catechetical implementation) characterize the 1970s and 1980s. Yet, even if these "forms" of the crisis have changed in part, their effects persist today, and Father de Lubac's discernment remains illuminating. He still has a grasp of the present reality.[3]

[2] See below, pp. 115–16. [The French translation of Jaki's book, to which the author here refers, was published in 1983.—TRANS.]

[3] See Hans Urs von Balthasar, *Theo-Drama: Theological Dramatic Theory*, vol. 4, *The Action*, trans. Graham Harrison (San Francisco: Ignatius Press, 1994), p. 460: "The situation of the Church herself, however, her heart invaded by a disintegrating rationalism, is certainly eminently dramatic. The situation is somewhat similar to Irenaeus' campaign against Gnosticism, but it is more acute insofar as the gnostic sects that claim to have the correct interpretation are no longer outside the Church: they are inside her, claiming to have the proper scientific tools and to be in authentic communication with all religions and world views. What an advantage over conservative orthodoxy, enclosed in its particularist dogmas and relying on obsolete traditions!"

Moreover, in the hands of our author, paradox seeks to free events or thoughts from their circumstantial clothing and to show the life of the spirit in them, whether it be welcomed or disputed. Instead of dozing off in the world of appearances or falling asleep in the emptiness of non-being, paradox helps the spirit awaken to the reality of things, which is its realm, and names the lie.

Father de Lubac had already trained himself in this particular form of exercise in his *Paradoxes* and *New Paradoxes*. It would have been regrettable not to have made these *Other Paradoxes* available to the public. They attest to our author's unceasing activity and form what is undoubtedly the most personal part of his work.[4] In addition, the reader will find in them the clarity, magnificent language, spiritual understanding, and shrewd discernment of Henri de Lubac.

For all these reasons, which its board of directors has deemed judicious, and also encouraged by friends of Father de Lubac, Culture et Vérité is publishing these *Other Paradoxes*. In doing so, all that was needed

---

[4] Cf. Hans Urs von Balthasar, "Une Oeuvre organique", in Hans Urs von Balthasar and Georges Chantraine, *Le Cardinal Henri de Lubac: L'Homme et son oeuvre* (Paris-Namur: Lethielleux-Culture et Vérité, 1983), pp. 117–21; Georges Chantraine, "Paradoxe et mystère: Logique théologique chez Henri de Lubac", in *Nouvelle revue théologique* 115 (1993): 543–59. Father de Lubac himself left in his memoir only the dozen descriptive lines just quoted about the *Paradoxes*. We do note, however, two other articles on this subject: M. Léna, "La Sainteté de l'intelligence", *Communio* 103 (1992): 81–89, and J. F. Thomas, "La Vérité du paradoxe", *Communio* 103 (1992): 92–109.

was a final revision: verifying references and quotations, eliminating a few repetitions, shifting one or two paradoxes for the sake of the beauty of the form, and, rarely, dropping a passage in the interests of discretion. My warm thanks go to my colleagues Fathers Jean-Marie Hennaux, Marc Leclerc, Louis Renard, and Henri Tihon for their work on this.

George Chantraine, S.J.
Rector of the Theology Faculty
Lugano

I

Gospel

This is hardly a paradox: The unsophisticated reader of the Gospels, unfamiliar with the details of the historical, social, political, and religious circumstances of the little Jewish, Galilean world in which Jesus lived, is perhaps in a better position to understand the heart of the Gospel than many a scholarly specialist. The latter, even if he is a believer, often has great difficulty seeing in what way precisely the message of Jesus, wholly rooted as it is in this particular locality, is of a supreme universality.

The divine simplicity of the Gospel is a divine complexity, like that of God himself. Starting from an a priori, a dogmatic or methodological a priori, whether explicit or implicit and at times even unperceived by themselves, many critics are guided by the idea that the person of Jesus does not transcend the limits of a human being conditioned by his surroundings. They are led in that way to select certain traits, and to eliminate others, so as to obtain a credible portrait. As von Balthasar has shown (*The Glory of the Lord*, vol. 1: *Seeing the Form* [San Francisco, New York: Ignatius Press, 1982], pp. 605–6), the result is merely a series of oversimplified outlines, skimpy representations, none of which has anything left but the semblance of a banal personality, and all of which contradict each other. Moreover, despite a desire to work an "objective" historical reconstruction, these forms often bear characteristics that could have been predicted in advance on the basis of the author's philosophy or mentality and the reconstruction of his period.

Jesus' central assertion, the assertion that he is "unique", that he is "the Son", has no relation to the culture of his time, to the Semitic culture any more than to the Hellenic culture. "Scandal for the Jews, folly for the Gentiles." This assertion would have to be refuted as senseless in order to reduce "Christianity", however one tries to explain it, to the relativity of a "cultural fact", as extensive as one might well admit this fact to be throughout space and time.

Nor do I do see this assertion of Jesus about himself, with all the gravity, all the demands, and all the consequence it entails, ever expressed by another human being at any other point in space or time.

I am prepared to follow, insofar as I am able, in any case with patience and docility, all the analyses, all the critical and philological explanations of our exegetes concerning each of the Gospels and each of their verses, their direct or indirect relationships, the reconstruction of their sources, the alterations of their texts, and so on, and so on. But I would first of all like to assure myself, in the course of a very simple exchange, without any artifice or technical jargon, that they have understood something about the Gospel as we have it in our hands today, in its fourfold form.

I hear talk everywhere about the *divergences* among the theologies of the authors of the New Testament. As for me, I admire much more their *convergence*.

✤

"There is indeed only one Christ in the New Testament, but there are many Christologies" (H. Zahrnt, *Dieu ne peut pas mourir*, trans. A. Liefooghe [Paris: Cerf, 1971], p. 183). Let us pass over the word "many", which is obviously excessive. Without contradicting the author, it would be better to turn his phrase around: "There are several Christologies in the New Testament, but there is only one Christ." Still, this adversative "but" is inadequate, for these various

Christologies do not contradict each other: they converge, they unite to give us a glimpse of the one Christ.

What is surprising about the fact that each author had his particular perspective? And how would a single perspective suffice? From the very first generation, Christians have understood this well.

When it is a question of setting the evangelists against each other, a discerning exegete has us note that Matthew on two occasions corrects Mark's text by saying (Mt 21:6 and 26:19) that "the disciples did what Jesus had told them": an obvious indication, he tells us, that Matthew is thereby telling the communities what they should do, which is to obey their leaders. And then, when a monograph is devoted to Matthew in a publication on first-century ministries, no allusion is made to these two passages, for the author has a completely different concern in mind: that of showing that all authority, or at least all authoritarianism, was absent from the "ancient Church", where only horizontal, "fraternal" relationships and various "ministries" were known.

Our exegetes look for intentions everywhere without perceiving that they themselves, in their would-be objective criticism, are directed too much by their own intention, or by that of the milieu influencing them.

⚜

To read some critics, it would seem that for them "redactional activity" means not only "intention" but "invention". It would seem that for them any page that is not insipid and colorless, superficial, without thought or intention, is a page that is at the least tendentious and therefore deceptive as well.

As moderate a critic as Günther Bornkamm continually tells us of the "retrospective testimony of the later community", of the "community [that] has participated in formulating the tradition", of "the interpretation of faith", of the "evangelists who worked out the scene", of "the tradition [that] erased, on many occasions, the difference existing between Jesus himself and the Son of man", and so on (*Qui est Jésus de Nazareth?*, French trans. [Paris: Seuil, 1973], pp. 27, 60, 63, 186, 201). All expressions with more or less flexible meanings that might correspond to reality. But the tendency is excessive when it ends in concluding that some remark or account is "not authentic" and a "creation of the community". The author perceives this himself, since he wisely warns us that such expressions "are not to be taken in a strict sense". But why, then, adopt them? The fact remains that for him, as for many others, "critical" is always vaguely synonymous with "negative". It would be nice, too, to have a little criticism—which would probably also be rather "negative"—exercised on this myth of the creative community. Bornkamm is right to say (p. 33) that tradition "ignores the boundary between history and its meaning", but he seems to see a defect in that, as if, quite to the contrary, a history without meaning were not necessarily reductive. Moreover, he suspects as much, since he adds, plunging us back into equivocation, that "it is precisely this way of talking about Jesus that brings out what is incomparably unique and particular about his person and his acts."

Bornkamm furthermore tells us that he wants, with respect to Jesus, "to apply a rigorous criticism in order to isolate in actual fact what, prior to any interpretation of faith, is offered to us unaltered and original" (p. 63). How do we not conclude from this that faith alters reality?

He quotes the passage from Mark 1:22: "He taught them as one who had authority", and provides this commentary: "This term 'authority' surely encloses the whole mystery of Jesus' person and influence, such as it is grasped by faith; it therefore transcends everything that is purely 'historical'." How can we not conclude that the mention of this authority of Jesus by the evangelists does not have any historical value? A true historian, following the criterion set by a "rigorous criticism", would therefore have had to write: "He taught them as one who did not have authority." Yet Bornkamm adds: this term authority "expresses a reality that, from its origin, belongs, before any interpretation, to the historical Jesus" (p. 71). Well then?

⚜

"One must see the thing all at once, in a single glance" (Pascal). This necessity does not condemn slow steps and meticulous groundwork. But such approaches are in vain, they can even obstruct one's vision, if they do not end in this "single glance". Many "critical" minds are unable to bring themselves to do this. They are like specialists of the eyes, the forehead, the nose, the mouth, the chin, the hair, the ears, the skin, and so on, who would *never* think of looking at the face from the required distance.

"Look at things from a greater distance and with a more penetrating gaze": that is the advice given by a scholar who is a meticulous analyst, Jean Ladrière (*La Science, le monde et la foi* [Tournai: Casterman, 1972], p. 96).

⚜

The First Letter of Paul to the Thessalonians. The first Christian writing. For the first time, the Christian tone resounds in our ears. There had been nothing like it up till then anywhere in the world. An unparalleled innovation in the history of man. And one that has nothing in common with any kind of literature, art, or thought. Everything has reference to the person of Jesus, everything originates in the event of Jesus. Paul knows, with invincible certainty, that this event has overturned everything, that everything begins with it. There is so much of the freshness of dawn, of new momentum, and already so much richness: organized churches, fraternal bonds between them, a concern for imitating Mother Church and for union with her, a community already of trials and persecutions—and this intense feeling of all life being changed, renewed in depth—and the great Apostle who is nothing, who wants to be nothing, beyond his testimony, but on whom his testimony confers an unparalleled authority: the authority of a father, of a mother, with all the tender love of father and mother. Without any didacticism, in a few appropriate pages, in a family letter, already what fullness, what doctrinal penetration: the first Christian lines, the prelude to this ocean of the past nineteen centuries—and all Christian life at once defined, summed up, forever, in the three theological virtues: faith, charity, hope: the threefold arrangement, the threefold face of one and the same life, which all comes from the divine election and which nonetheless calls forth effort, activity, resolute tension in the Christian: ἔργου τῆς πίστεως, κόπου τῆς ἀγάπης, ὑπομονῆς τῆς ἐλπίδος, "work of faith, labor of love, and steadfastness of hope" (1 Thess 1:3). It is the Holy Spirit who animates everything and who spreads joy in the midst of tribulations. There is nothing of an idyll in these beginnings: no easy ways, nothing bland; everywhere, already, the struggle has begun: the preaching of the Gospel is carried out ἐν πολλῷ ἀγῶνι "in the face of great opposition" (1 Thess 2:2), and the men who withstand this opposition with Paul are a handful of worthless men. But this is in reality the victorious struggle of the "living and true God" against all the evil forces without and all the idols of the heart; of the God who gives rise to the movement of all being toward him: ἡ πίστις ὑμῶν ἡ πρὸς θεόν "your faith in God" (1 Thess 1:8), in awaiting his Son Jesus, whom he has raised from the dead. From Paul to this little nascent community, from the Thessalonians to their father, there is a constant exchange of remembrance in prayer; with his very first words, Paul alludes to it, and this custom survives even to this day in the Church between Christians who correspond. Each one is thus strengthened by all so as to go forward in everything in a way worthy of the God who calls them all to share his Kingdom and his glory. This is not some abstract idea; neither is it unrealistic. We sense here already the threat of disputes, illusions, schisms. Paul, unable to come himself, sends his dear Timothy to witness, of course, to his love for his children, but also to see to the good order of the community, to quell budding conflicts, to assure the unity within it and with the other churches. For the weight of what is all "too human" always, and often very quickly, causes lapses, and the Tempter is always at work, threatening to render the entire work of the Apostle futile . . .

I am not consulting a commentary. The simple reading of this letter, a reading without any scholarly pretensions, provided it is slow and careful, is enough to make one feel the weight of the words, the density of the expressions, the overturning of the old man, the radical newness, and this new atmosphere of pure joy and radiant hope. It is like the Christmas of Christian literature . . . And all that, for anyone who consents to open himself to it, is as new today as it ever was. And none of that without *Jesus*, whom the evangelists, coming from sister communities, make known to us, not by overestimating his importance, as blind "critics" as well as scholars claim, but, on the contrary, with an evident powerlessness to express what they feel in their hearts: the unique grandeur, strength, and newness of the person and work of Jesus.

The Gospels are not biographies but testimonies of faith. This is quite certain, provided one does not make the antithesis rigid (for a testimony of faith is not a preconceived theology, and biographical elements belong to it in an essential way). But does anyone believe that, were they biographies and not testimonies of faith, the Gospels would teach us better about Jesus?

"We have to pass through the faith of the primitive community"; consequently, "how are we to attain the historical Jesus of Nazareth in his reality?" But how else would one wish to go if not by way of this faith? Is it not the best route? If the companions of Jesus had not had faith in him, how would they have made him known to us? They might well have given us (let us imagine) all sorts of exact details about his deeds and gestures, his comings and goings, and so on: In what respect could that have been of interest to us?

So that I might legitimately believe in Jesus, they would have him made known to me by men who themselves did not believe in him! The apostles would be valid witnesses only if they had not wished to give witness.

They endlessly bring up what they call "the major difficulty" about Jesus: "We reach Jesus only through the faith of his disciples." This "only" seems strange to me. Through what would they prefer to reach Jesus? Through the testimony of those who were indifferent, skeptical? Do they suppose that such testimony would have more value? In order to judge that the faith of the witness constitutes, as such, suspect testimony, one would have to suppose a priori that Jesus did not merit that faith. That is a *petitio principii*.

Every page of the Gospels is skillfully explained to me. This comes, I am told, from the liturgy of a community; that comes from catechesis; this comes from the reaction against a dissident trend; that comes from the theology of such and such an evangelist, and so on. All that is very ingenious, and it is sometimes true, or at least probable. But in the end, one cannot avoid the question: Where did this liturgy come from? Where did that catechesis, that reaction come from? Who had gathered this community together? What was the source of that theology? When one has spoken of "creativity", has one explained anything? Is "creativity" a pure creation? And if one must grant it a part, is it not that part which it must have as the unavoidable means of conserving the whole living reality? In brief, would the best explanation still not be the simplest, that which relates everything to Jesus and to the impression he made on the Twelve? Without seeking some impossible literalism, is it not best for me, therefore, to start reading the *Gospel* again ingenuously?

Today each makes, contrary to the Jesus of the Church, a Jesus according to his own taste: an Essene Jesus, a Zealot Jesus, a Gnostic Jesus, a visionary Jesus, a pre-Marxist Jesus, a Jesus who denies the Father . . . There is no reason to be surprised by this. But it is fallacious and deceptive to place this current "pluralism" on the same footing with the pluralism of the portraits of Jesus offered us by his first witnesses. What could there be in common between this jumble of the most eccentric points and the varied, but in reality convergent, points of view by which Mark, Luke, Matthew, Paul, and John present the one Jesus to us? The fact that one stresses the idea of "Messiah", another the idea of "Son of Man", another that of "Servant of

Yahweh", and so forth, does not set them in contradiction to each other. And if Jesus is indeed what each of them, in his own way, tells us, must we not conclude from that precisely that it was impossible to make him known to us except through such a diversity of viewpoints? If he was coming truly to fulfill the whole hope of Israel, by transfiguring it, was it not necessary to show that these great, contradictory images all found their utmost unity in the unique personality of Jesus? And could that be done otherwise than through a series of approaches in which one would have to be myopic not to see that each combines not only to enrich the same portrait but to authenticate the same Face?

The miniature Bultmanns who are proliferating among us might be invited to make at least a modest place in their "critical" reconstructions of the formation of the Gospels, alongside the lofty speculations about the "creativity" of the primitive community and about the theological biases of each evangelist, for the well-attested humble fact that in the milieu in which Jesus taught, a good disciple was recognized as being "like a well-built cistern that does not lose a drop".

Reasonable critics, dazzled by their discovery, announce to us that we are victims of a great historical error. The Church, in reality, was not founded by Jesus. No trace of any written proof of her foundation is found anywhere at her origins: not the least charter, not the least notarized document, not the least constituent assembly.

These critics are indeed correct: The Church was not founded as a new State or as an industrial firm or as a commercial society or as an early anticipation of the UN. The Church was *born* of Jesus. She was born of his Passion and his Resurrection; she was born of the Spirit whom he himself sent. And Jesus had prepared her, he had formed her first nucleus. What the evangelists preserve for us about the selection of the Twelve, their education, their mission, their initiation into the divine life, about the investiture of Peter, and so forth, all that cannot be dismissed en bloc.

The Church is at once visible and invisible, a mysterious reality and a society made up of people. Born and founded. A living organism and an edifice that has been constructed. It is useless to seek to eliminate one of these two aspects in favor of the other; it is impossible to reduce the complexity of the reality and dismiss the paradox. The whole endeavor to conceive of the Church according to any human model whatever is pointless. In her origins as in her present reality, she is always *other*, unique.

A whole host of exegetes, full of knowledge and "critical" industriousness, find a thousand ways, in their analyses, to persuade themselves that the individual Jesus was only some insubstantial being, some narrow-minded scribe or other, an enlightened prophet, or one politician among others, indeed, a party chief unduly magnified by unfaithful disciples. And yet here, after nineteen centuries, a man feels the need to set what he calls his "gay science" in opposition to the "good news". Nietzsche sees no other adversary worthy of him but Jesus. Even in his madness, how much more clear-sighted he was than all these new scribes!

In measuring himself against Jesus, in seeking to imitate him in a mixture of admiration and contempt, of hatred and love, Nietzsche still gave witness to him. He was not criticizing his doctrine, he was measuring himself against a living being. He did not treat him like some distant philosopher; it would not have occurred to him to discuss him as one discusses Aristotle or Plato—or even as one discusses Socrates, whom he saw as the one chiefly to be blamed. Jesus, for him, was a living Person.

One often sees disciples, even right after the death of the master, lower his ideal, materialize it, substitute the paltriest conceptions for his intentions, and so forth. Disciples have never been seen—unless one believes certain "critical" historians with reference to Jesus—to transform illusory, wholly earthly views totally dependent on his time and place into this extraordinary body of sublime doctrines, formed into a living organism, capable of penetrating everywhere in order to transform souls, of inspiring the sense of a unique Newness and of cutting across centuries—all that without there being, at the very root, the least perceptible protestation on the part of the very first disciples, the least concern of any of them to reestablish the true doctrine of their master. Rather, quite to the contrary, those disciples accuse themselves, right from the beginning, of having often understood that doctrine poorly, entangled as they were in their petty dreams, their carnal views and those of all around them; which earned them a good rebuke from him.

I readily admit that many of the words attributed to Jesus by the evangelists derive, in the form in which we know them, from the evangelists themselves or from their milieu. I will even suppose for a moment (an unimaginable thing!) that they not only adapted and elaborated on them but also invented them. We would then be faced with an unheard-of event, unparalleled in history. What extraordinary witnesses, capable of inventing, each on his own, such things that, for long centuries, were destined to overturn minds and hearts, to fulfill the tradition of Israel by seeming to destroy it, to introduce into the old civilization a spiritual leaven that would transform it completely—and all agreeing to attribute everything to someone else, to that very Jesus they all considered, across the diversity of their intentions, to be their unique Master and Lord: they were themselves the authors of this unparalleled Newness, which, as they show us despite themselves and by so many signs, they had so poorly understood!

It is quite right to tell us that the Gospels are not "mere reports, neutral and impartial", that the presentation of the documents made use of by the evangelists has been "modeled by faith". This is so obvious, there is no need endlessly to remind us of it. "Gospel, Good News" (Mk 1:1): that is neither neutral nor impartial. These things were written "that you may believe that Jesus is the Christ, the Son of God" (Jn 20:31): there is no pretense in that. But if we assume—and this hypothesis cannot be excluded a priori—that the events themselves called for faith and that, consequently, a mere "neutral" report would have been misleading or at least incomplete, how could this report be called "impartial"?

We are also told that the Gospels give us with respect to Jesus' ministry a "description that goes beyond the historical reality". I see here as well that such an expression can have some truth to it; it is very clear that Mark and the others are interpreters, that they transmit to us something other than an account of "dry facts". How could it be otherwise? The "historical reality" of Jesus' ministry can certainly not be reduced to "dry facts". It can be made understandable only through interpretations. But why decide that these interpretations transport us "beyond"? Perhaps it would be better justified to say that they leave us still "this side" of it.

Why distinguish between "the level of history and that of the Gospel", as if the first were below the second? Would the evangelists, then, have supposedly embellished and enlarged Jesus? In that case, how could their faith, our faith, be justified? If the apostolic preaching "considerably magnified" the Jesus of history, which is to say, the true Jesus, would we not have to conclude from that that it created an illusion (or, one used to say, a deception [*une tromperie*])? If we consider the fruits that this apostolic preaching has borne, would it not be infinitely more probable that it conveyed him, in the end, in his profound meaning, which is to say, in his substance? "New shading", they add; but why would this "new shading" not be more true than the first? How many times has experience not shown us that men understand nothing of the scenes they witness?

Besides, as one might well suspect in advance: the "translation" of an event of great spiritual importance inevitably entails, to the very degree of that importance, explanations that cannot always be produced at the moment. Memory is in this instance often more sure, more penetrating than the first perception. In other words, is there not some naïveté on the part of exegetes, who claim to be critical, upon discovering what they call "redactional layers", in persuading themselves that each of these "layers" enlarged on the reality and in consequence distorted it? Can any transcription of a reality that is at once historical and spiritual (and is the "Jesus event" not the eminent case of such a reality?) be made in any other way except through "redactional layers"?

⚜

For someone who thinks that the Christian reality bursting forth in history was only one phenomenon among others, without profound interest, without extreme consequences, it might seem natural to think that the wild imaginings, the exaggerations, the illusions of a few exalted groups ("creations of the community"), shaped by a few more or less doctrinaire writers, were enough to engender that reality. Or rather, we would have to admit the paradox that the individual Jesus was only a pretext for the sudden appearance of this reality, the greatest (even to human sight) that history offers us. Others, going "beyond", would supposedly be the true authors.

Origen's remark is still true: "But how can a phantom deceiver, once gone, do such works?" (*Contra Celsus* 7, 35; cf. 3, 44).

⚜

The search for the intentions of an author can help one understand him, to discover a certain order at first unperceived in his thought or in the very plan of his work. So we must, for example, take into account certain statements made or at least certain hypotheses expressed with respect to the place given to Peter in the third Gospel: when Luke, one observes, speaks of Jesus calling Simon, he is preparing the ground: "He is already thinking of the prominent role he is going to give to Peter" in Acts. When he then mentions

Jesus' prayer for Peter during the Last Supper, it is again "a similar literary preparation". When he finally alludes to the appearance of the risen Lord to Simon, it is "perhaps, once again, in order to prepare" for what he is going to say in the book of Acts "about the important role played by Peter at the beginning of the life of the Church".

Yes, "perhaps". But even if all that were assured, no firm conclusion could be drawn from it for or against the historicity of the three facts reported by Luke. But who does not see that a certain way of explaining everything in the text by the "intentions" of the author ends in identifying everything as "inventions"? It is very clear that a writer is not a machine. He has his own personality. He has, as they say, his "centers of interest". He does not write anything without an intention. Consciously or not, he always chooses his subject, the features he wants to emphasize, the order that seems to him the most logical or the most significant, the details he prefers to others, the words even. But we still need to know if all these mental and redactional operations are placed at the service of the real object to be explained or if they tend to present it under a false light, to transform it, indeed, in the final analysis, to substitute an unreal object for it. Now, by carrying intentions to the point of fanaticism, by seeking to explain everything by means of them, critics succeed in seeing only them; they end, then, by giving the impression that everything in the work studied depends on the subjectivity of the writer and seem to annul all objectivity.

⚜

Certain critical subtleties, whose ingeniousness is incontestable, furnish a good illustration of the proverb that says we need to keep from putting the cart before the horse.

How, for example, are we to explain what the fourth Gospel reports about the mysterious "disciple whom Jesus loved"? This could be achieved without too much difficulty if we were able to discern the intentions of the redactor, which is to say, the interests of those for whom he is the spokesman. Now, "in the eyes of the Johannine community", the beloved disciple certainly represented "the basic source to which one referred in speaking about Jesus (Jn 19:35), and he had a right to the greatest respect. It was therefore very important that he appear close to the Master during the crucial events whose account had become the most precious legacy of the Christian tradition, which is to say, the Last Supper, the Passion, the crucifixion, and the consequences of the Resurrection."

In other words, everything that is recounted about the beloved disciple is only fiction, intended not even to establish but rather to explain his authority after the fact. No one wonders for an instant where his authority might have come from. They do not consider the very normal hypothesis that, if he was regarded as "the basic source . . .", it was perhaps quite simply because he might truly have been the friend of Jesus, present at the "crucial events".

Napoleon was admired in the nineteenth century as

a great general. That is why tradition attributed to him the victories at the bridge of Arcole, Austerlitz, Jena, Wagram. There is no point in wondering if, by chance, it was the reality of these victories that might have assured him the reputation of being a great general.

To read certain exegetes, one first principle is supposedly indisputable: Anything in the Gospels that goes beyond the most insipid banality could not be from Jesus. One wonders why the evangelists themselves should have been less insipid, why it should always be necessary to judge them—or the "community" for which they are the spokesmen—superior to Jesus.

In the work of establishing a text, as all the critics know, the *lectio difficilior* is generally the best. But for the incompetent reader, for the lazy, for the one who does not reflect, it is the *lectio facilior* that prevails.

The *lectio difficilior* of the universe is the one that faith suggests. The satisfaction it brings, without ever being an end in itself, clearly reveals the illusory character of all the overly facile readings invented by man.

The same is true for the Fact of Christ. It is much easier to reduce it to everyday banalities, to diminish it to ready-made "models", to interpret it according to the probabilities that common experience suggests—assuredly easier than to recognize in it the irreducible Fact, outside of any analogy as well as of any probability, any "reasonable" expectation, any explanation that does not threaten or disturb our habits or thwart our passions. Easier than to admit that one is coming up against something unique and that no reductive effort will succeed. Now precisely there is the *lectio difficilior* that reflection makes imperative.

For the author of the Letter to the Hebrews, "the Christian interpretation of the Old Testament is quite obviously essential. The biblical texts have, so to speak, been drawn by Christ as filings are drawn by a magnet. They have come to be applied to the mystery of Jesus and can no longer be detached from him. They have found their definitive meaning" (Albert Vanhoye, *Situation du Christ: Hébreux 1–2* [Paris: Cerf, 1969], p. 123).

This could be said as well, for example, of Saint John—and of the whole Christian tradition. And it is the principle of the utter timelessness of the ancient Scripture for the faith of the Christian.

"To select from the New Testament certain passages which seem to have a 'modern' ring, and to declare that these represent the 'permanent element' in it, is not necessarily to preach the Gospel" (Charles H. Dodd, *The Apostolic Preaching and Its Developments* [New York and Evanston: Harper and Row, 1964], p. 78).

Some believe they are obliged to "pick out in the New Testament what is 'still' acceptable 'today'. The natural thoughtlessness with which this criterion is accepted seems to me one of the most dangerous symptoms of the mentality that reigns among young theologians today. If they subordinate theology to the spirit of the century and to experience viewed as criteria, theological activity is no longer anything but wind" (Hans Conzelmann, *Théologie du Nouveau Testament*, trans. Étienne de Peyer [Geneva: Labor et Fides, 1969], p. 8).

"The words of Jesus Christ. Are they words like any others? Sublime childishness? The expression of fanaticism, such as we see in late Judaism or with the Essenes? The inventions of a community of believers who placed such marvelous words in the mouth of its master after the fact? (What a superior community, if that were the case: what a creative group!)—But perhaps none of all that explains these words; perhaps the one who speaks in his solitude is someone who confronts in all tranquility any contradiction whatsoever, who does not rely in any respect on his successors (whom he does enlist and send, however), who does not enter a competition on any point with the wise men, the philosophers, the theologians, or the mystics of any peoples or any times, he who is more simple and more public, more secret and more esoteric than any of them. It is not only the doctrine contained in these words that will hold the world's attention to the end, but it is the man who articulated it. Who can he be, this man who says: 'Heaven and earth will pass away, but my word will not pass away'? Words that any Greek, any humanist would have to term extreme presumptuousness and yet that emanate from the most humble of men. Who is he? The encounter with him is unavoidable. In comparison, the time spent in bothering about problematic aspects of the Church is time wasted. . . . We quibble over trifles, because we are afraid to confront what is of first importance. The Mystery is there, in this man; we cannot long avoid it. The circuitous path we oblige ourselves to take every day is fatiguing in the long run. We will have to just make our way straight toward the Center, who knows how to wait" (Hans Urs von Balthasar, "Religion et culture chrétiennes dans le monde actuel", *Comprendre: Revue de la Société européene de culture* 17–18 [Venice, 1957]; reproduced[1] in *Nouveaux points de repère*, Communio [Paris: Fayard, 1980], pp. 354–55).

[1] [It was Father de Lubac who suggested to Father H. U. von Balthasar that he add this article, which was important in his opinion, to the collection published by Father G. Chantraine. The text quoted here differs in a few words from that published in *Nouveaux points de repère*.]

⚜

"The word of a great poet is not vulnerable to philological criticism: it is what it is; it acts as it is, without concerning itself with the praise or the blame of philologists. The praise and the blame will pass away, the word of Goethe will not pass away. In the same way, and even more so, the Word of God is elevated above all exegesis that helps or hinders it, all analytical or systematic exegesis; it accepts these efforts, but they will pass away, while the Word remains" (Hans Urs von Balthasar, *Das Ganze im Fragment: Aspekte der Geschichtstheologie* [Einsiedeln: Benziger Verlag, 1963], p. 264; American ed.: *A Theological Anthropology* [New York: Sheed and Ward, 1967]).

II

Council. Collegiality. Para- and Post-Council

"Most of the measures for renewal are so influenced by a simple reaction against the past that I fear disaster." Letter from a Brother of Taizé sent from Chicago to Roger Schutz (R. Schutz, *Violence des pacifiques* [Presses de Taizé, 1968], pp. 75–76).

"It is a great pity when a century comes to admire itself and to place itself naïvely above everything that was" (Lamennais, *Pensées diverses. Oeuvres* [1844] 7:379).

The Congregation for the Doctrine of the Faith recalls several elementary Catholic truths about the Magisterium of the Church and about the Catholic priesthood, referring in particular, very precisely, to

Vatican II: the next day the Swiss journals compare this act to the invasion of Czechoslovakia by Soviet tanks.

There is a lot of talk about the "Church of Vatican II". And also about the "Church of Pius X", the "Church of Trent", or the "Church of Paul VI". There is an abuse of language in that. It is a way of emphasizing discontinuities, of exaggerating them, indeed, of imagining ruptures, of making too much of contingent, secondary traits to the detriment of the essential, which endures. It is to forget that the councils and the popes, in the exercise of their authority, are only the servants of the Christian tradition. I know only one Church, the Church of all time, the Church of Jesus Christ, the Church of the apostles, the history of which is certainly very eventful, but which is never renewed except in order to remain herself.

Another expression that has become a catchword nowadays is detestable in the way it is understood and in the conclusions drawn from it; "Vatican II", it is said, "is not a point of arrival but a starting point." It is, to be sure, a starting point, in the sense that the texts were written in order to be applied and to bear their sometimes unforeseen fruit. But, on the one hand, they are not an absolute starting point, as if they were canceling out nineteen centuries of tradition that they continue; on the other hand, it is a betrayal of the Council to consider it like an open door to something else and virtually to repudiate it in both letter and spirit on the pretext, as is sometimes said, of "going farther".

They no longer trouble themselves, henceforth, with the content of the Council; they consider it to be the transitory effect of a compromise between an elite group, conscious of the true needs of the hour but unable to lead the whole flock in its footsteps, and the backward members of that flock. To it must go the credit, they say, for having "opened a breach", for having "begun a transformation".

Another expression is also altogether excessive. *Lumen gentium* supposedly worked a "Copernican revolution" by defining the Church as the "People of God", while up to then she had been considered a hierarchy.

That is a bad cliché; in those simplistic terms, it is a historical error. The expression was launched as a triumphal cry by theologians who in all innocence imagined themselves to have played a role greater than it was and who lost all sense of proportion.

On the one hand, for centuries, the most commonly known definitions, in large treatises as well as in little catechisms, have characterized the Church as an assembly of believers, united to their bishop and, through him, to the pope, and thus forming a society that is one and universal;[1] this was not, of course, an

[1] It continues to be said and written generally that, up to the present, theologians and catechists defined the Church solely by

exhaustive definition (neither is there one in Vatican II), but Vatican II did not reverse it. On the other hand, it is not true that the Council "defined" the Church as the people of God. *Lumen gentium* teaches first of all, and at length, that the Church is a mystery, so much a mystery that essential aspects will always elude any attempt at a definition restricted to a single formula; it then explains that her reality is expressed in Scripture through images, among which that of the "Body of Christ" holds a privileged position. It passes only then to the image of the "People of God", which will provide its principal perspective; but it does not understand this "People" in a temporal, ethnic, social, or political sense, nor does it conceive it as an undifferentiated mass. In the following chapters, it analyzes the different elements of this people by speaking of the pastors, which is to say the bishops united to the pope and assisted by their priests, and then the laity. There is nothing revolutionary about that.

It is said, again, that "the Council worked a very profound change in the theology of the Church since it refused to define her first of all as a hierarchical society and considered her first of all as a people." A very profound change worked like this in a dogmatic

---

means of the "hierarchy" or "in a clerical way". I see the contrary everywhere. "Ecclesia, id est catholicorum collectio"; or "Congregatio fidelium"; or "Universitas christianorum", etc. It is the same in the French catechisms. It is then mentioned, of course, that the Christian is subject to the legitimate pastors, which the New Testament was already teaching.

constitution could only have been a betrayal of the faith of the Church. Such excesses of language could only justify the integrist groups who claim that Vatican II fell into heresy. But in reality, if one speaks in a broad sense of "definition", one should say that the Council defined the Church *first of all* as the Body of Christ, and not without specifying above all that she is a mystery and that no concept, no image can suffice to express this mystery. It is next forgotten that to speak of the people of God is not to "define the Church as a people"; the omission of "God" in this expression is a serious one—obviously not because its author, who is a bishop, intended to exclude him—but because by confining oneself to the word "people", one no longer suggests taking it in the analogical and specific sense that it has in Christian language (both in continuity with and in opposition to the ancient people of Israel). And the phrase quoted above inevitably suggests the contrary of what the Council said and the order in which it said it.

Two remarks come back to me. One was made by a very plainspoken, straightforward Protestant pastor, who said to me one day: "You Catholics have betrayed the truth, but you have the Church, the one Church." The other was by an Orthodox prelate who, after having said to me: "The union of Christians must be accomplished, and it is clear that it can be done only around the pope of Rome", added, in a sad voice, "but we are disconcerted to see that the authority of the pope is presently contested within Catholicism, and that is going to delay union very much."

"I am frightened", writes one bishop, "to note the facility with which anyone can write anything on points that touch the very substance of our faith and the essential structure of the Church without provoking anything but some 'prudent' clarifications that do nothing but add to the perplexity of Christians who want to be faithful."

In my mail, this letter from a lay person: ". . . There are churches one cannot enter without a feeling of coldness and emptiness, where the Mass seems to be the work of two or three chatterboxes assisted by a bored and resigned priest, seated in his corner; he barely wakes up for a moment to go deliver an approximate canon, then slip away. . . . Our parish passes for a "traditionalist" one. . . . Yet they are giving in to that obsession with criticism without any discernment of the past, with enthusiasm for the 'great things' that are going to be accomplished and that seem only like vague good intentions. There is hardly a sermon that does not end with this formula: 'In the past, it was said, it was believed that, and so on. Now it has finally been realized that, and so on.'

This is a little annoying, because I recognize the teaching that I have always received in these so-called discoveries, and not at all in what is attributed to the 'old Church'. I find the errors and abuses of a few hotheads much less serious than the sheeplike spirit of most of our 'good clerics', who are afraid of being thought behind the times, who tolerate what they disapprove, attribute everything that is bad in the world to the faults of the Church, and seek 'gimmicks' borrowed from social psychology to 'catch the masses', 'follow the world', and so on. These 'gimmicks', for prayers just as for the press and the radio, are mediocrity, vulgarity. And they don't even have the advantage of being successful!

"I do not know the secrets of that world. But our fine country priests, wherever they are, are rarely absent from a retreat, as formerly, but for 'reorientation', from which they return 'pumped up' like militants of some faction and speak with enthusiasm of the new Church without priests, with no connection to what used to be known by that name, and so on. Holy priests are not what is wanted any more, but effective, 'responsible' ones. . . . All that is painful. The very notion of the Church is obscured when bishops scarcely ever listen to the pope, pastors scarcely ever listen to their bishops, assistants scarcely ever listen to their pastors, when the least theologian sets himself up as a parallel authority and when each of these clerics claims to impose his own ideas and actions on the faithful. I am nonetheless bound to the Church of Peter, since Christ established her."

⚜

We had already welcomed *aggiornamento* wholeheartedly. We had already hoped for it, waited for it. Some had contributed to the preparations for it, before and during the Council. They were ready, right after the Council, to do their part, to put it into action, employing all their strength to do so. They thought that, despite the difficulties of the task, they would be sustained in it by the great collective effort required.

In order to remain faithful to the Council, they were obliged to follow this Yes that they said to the Council—and which they do not cease to say—with a No to the perversion that followed it—and an increasingly energetic No insofar as that the perversion got worse.

It is not a matter, then, as some say here and there rather tritely but falsely, of a divergence or an opposition between the timid and the bold, between moderates and extremists, between the audacious who go too quickly and the prudent whose progress is too slow, and so on. It is very clearly a matter of refusing the perversion. It is a matter of refusing to betray. For the Council is being betrayed, in its spirit as in its letter. What is being produced at the present time in the Church, in France, and what goes so far as to carry along (in blindness) even bishops and major superiors, is the opposite of what the Council wanted to encourage.

While the bishops were assembled in Rome around the pope, while the great conciliar texts were being worked out, some groups with convergent intentions were organized. A faction was formed, followed by much paraconciliar unrest. As always in such cases, most of those who were caught up in this unrest did not see, or saw poorly, where they were being led. But some determined minds knew what they wanted, radical "transformation", which is to say, the secularization of the Church, which is to say, by its true name, apostasy. It is apostasy that is covered up by the successive tinsel of the "spirit of the Council", "secularization", "pluralism", and so on. From year to year, hypocrisy gives way to cynicism, and there are still eyes that do not want to see.

Contrary to what the opponents of the Council said and to what Bishop Lefebvre still says on the subject of "religious freedom", contrary to what is conceded even by some warm partisans of the conciliar declaration, who appeal only to an older tradition, that of the very first centuries of the Church, there is no contradiction as claimed between that declaration and the Catholic opinion habitually held in the eighteenth and nineteenth centuries, an opinion that is expressed in certain Roman documents. Numerous religious writers of those two centuries made a clear distinction between the two senses, internal and external, of "tolerance", as they often say, and freedom. The first, doctrinal indifference, disdain for seeking the truth, the refusal of any norm for the conscience, was condemned; the second, civil and social, was, on the contrary, approved. In their condemnation of internal tolerance, or indifference, many depended on Pascal. The principal one among them was Lamennais, in his renowned *Essai sur l'indifférence*, but there were others before him, such as Xavier de Feller, Du Voisin, Bergier, Bonald, Frayssinous, Teysserre—whom Christian Maréchal quotes in *La Jeunesse de La Mennais* (Perrin, 1913), pp. 550–635. And such as Genoude, who took up Lamennais' defense on this subject.

That the Council did not start the process of "secularization" that is being pursued at the present time in the Church is proved by a page from Karl Barth, who observed the phenomenon (and not only in the Calvinist confession) in 1958–1959: he noted at that time "the internal secularization that is threatening the Church as such, her message, her doctrine, her order, and her mission". Some, he said, have attacked "the sterile, static difference between the *ecclesia docens* and the *ecclesia audiens*; but, in doing so, [they have called] into question the fruitful, dynamic sense of this difference, because by emphasizing the unholy priority of some human word, they have disputed the holy priority of the Word of God, and they have been more or less successful in getting rid of it. They have managed to say 'universal priesthood' while understanding thereby the sovereignty of the individual man or of the masses. They managed to brush aside priests, theologians, and preachers, even though in reality they were brushing aside the Lord of the whole Church. . . . While explaining and applying (but also criticizing!) the Bible and dogma, while calling on the Holy Spirit (who breathes where he wills) and the conscience before which each is directly responsible, they have managed in theory to highlight brotherhood in Christ, while in practice they have succeeded only in glorifying the thoughts, the words, and the life . . . of covetous *homunculi* [little men] and sought to make them reign in the midst of the Church herself. Moreover, if 'ecclesiastics' and theologians have frequently appeared so closed to the 'people', they have proved quite as often that they were far too weak and accommodating in their regard, capitulating very quickly to their 'desires', although what was at stake demanded that they be vigilant, firm, and sure guides."

"How many Christians there are with a very limited view of ecclesiastical history, giving free rein, in the face of tradition, to their meager good sense and their restless imagination, cheerfully simplifying the questions in their thirst for initiative. . . . [Their rush to influential positions] has opened wide the door to the most diverse errors and confusion, threatening in truth, not only an old or a new 'orthodoxy', but even the very understanding and progress of the Gospel" (K. Barth, *Dogmatique*, 4:3, trans. Ryser [Geneva: Labor et Fides, 1972], pp. 35–36; original German edition: 1959).

⚜

"It was 'by looking at herself in the mirror of the Gospel' that the Church began her *aggiornamento*; it is by entering into dialogue with the world that she will begin her Change. Would it not be by working a revolution as radical as that which transformed a Galilean sect, attached to a people and the Law of Moses, into a Church in which no distinction was made between either Jews or Greeks, pagans or free men or slaves, that Christianity, faithful to all the demands of its Founder's Law of love, would become for the entire world—whose language and aspirations it would have accepted and all of whose problems it would have assumed—the universal Church?" (*Aggiornamento ou Mutation?*, typed edition of September 1965, conclusion; a pamphlet of collected essays, published by Abbé Jean Heckenroth and Dr. J. Bavouzet, with the collaboration of the Rev. Fr. Morel and of M. Marcel Pobé, "who have used their respective abilities as philosopher and historian in an attentive revision of these pages").

⚜

O Deus, si hoc nostro tempore levare possemus capita nostra et videre quod appropinquaret redemptio nostra, quia videmus Ecclesiam numquam ad eum casum devenisse, in quo nunc est. "O God, if in this time that is ours we can raise our head and see that our redemption approaches, it is because we see that the Church has never fallen so low as she now is" (Nicolas of Cusa, *De concordantia catholica*, bk. 1, chap. 12).

"I believe that the trials that await us would terrify and bewilder hearts even as courageous as those of Saint Athanasius, Saint Gregory I, and Saint Gregory VII. The latter would recognize that, no matter how dark the prospect that overwhelmed them in their time, ours is in a kind of darkness different from all those that preceded it."

"The doctrines of the Fathers are scorned, the apostolic traditions are considered as nothing, the discoveries of innovators are greatly valued in the churches. Instead of being theologians, they have learned to be speculative. The wisdom of the world has the place of honor, having taken the place of the glory of the Cross" (Saint Basil, *Letter* 90).

New Integrism

How many people who think themselves "advanced" are lagging behind the real situation! They create for themselves a myth for today out of a reality that belongs to the day before yesterday. Real, effective, offensive integrism, the enemy of freedom, is no longer that of a group of sclerotic theologians, flanked by a few intriguers, influencing the Holy Office and the papacy itself: it is that of a group of "progressive" theologians, no less powerfully supported, influencing the new power, that of public opinion. At least as much courage is necessary to stand up to these latter as was necessary to resist the former. Moreover, a myth about the Roman Curia being finicky, obscurantist, made up of careerists with a complete disregard for the pastoral, and so forth, still prevails everywhere, now more than ever, in milieux that consider themselves enlightened—even though it is in the set of anti-establishment intellectuals (or pseudo-intellectuals) that one actually finds a failure to appreciate the realities of the Christian life and where tyrannical ideologies prevail; even though the Roman "authorities" are paralyzed; even though nearly all chief posts of the Curia are occupied by new men, who have been proven in pastoral ministry and who have played an effective role in bringing the Council to a successful conclusion; even though this Roman Curia is, proportionally, much more restrained than some national curias, and even though reception there is more simple and its spirit more open.... And if it is true that for a long time the faction that might be roughly designated as Roman, or as the orthodox (poorly understood) party, conducted rear-guard combat with at times dubious methods, today the situation has been reversed: one must be bold, stand up to public opinion, consent to being denigrated, accept even being silenced, resist new fads and a thousand compromises, if one wants to maintain the absolute of Christian revelation, the essence of Scripture, tradition, and the Church, which alone is capable of assuring the future of the faith.

⚜

"Perhaps, as one who lived through the Council and rejoiced at its work, I may be allowed to say here that there are phenomena in the life of the Church at the present moment which make me anxious to recall to the hearts of all of us that charismatic life is self-destructive in the long run, unless the divinely established rights of magisterial control are honestly recognized and loyally obeyed" (Christopher Butler, "Institution versus Charismata", in *Renewal of Religious Structures*, vol. 2 of *Theology of Renewal: Proceedings of the Congress on the Theology of the Renewal of the Church Centenary of Canada, 1867–1967* [New York: Herder and Herder, 1968], p. 54).

⚜

"The bishops receive their full power from Christ, not from the faithful; but as bishops, surrounded by the college of their priests, they are 'servants of God' (Rom 7:22) and 'servants of the community of faith' (see Eph 4:12)."

". . . In the general assembly of the Church, where the voices of other churches will be heard and to which Pope John XXIII wishes once again to call the bishops, according to the custom in Scripture" (*Lettre pastorale de l'épiscopat hollandais sur "Le sense du Concile"*, Utrecht, on Christmas Eve, 1960; French trans. [Paris, DDB], p. 39).

"It is not a council, it is Christ who has, through his Good News, caused the great change in the history of the world. The Church ceaselessly appeals to this unique act of salvation, accomplished once and for all, in her maternal care for our good" (ibid., p. 57).

"In many of the circles intoxicated with conciliar triumphalism, it has become impossible to speak of the ambiguity of the world . . . without being driven back into the outer darkness" (René Pascal, in *Esprit*, February 1967, p. 379).

"The *velamen* [veil] of the Jews is in the process of passing over to the Christians" (Léon Bloy, *Le Pèlerin de l'Absolu* [Paris: Mercure de France], p. 11. August 1910). Prophetic!

⚜

"It is rare for a council not to be followed by much confusion" (Newman, *Letter to the Duke of Norfolk* [1875]). [This quotation could not be located in the English editions of Newman—ED.]

⚜

"The final word has not been said about the *Nota praevia explicativa*, which has already caused much ink to flow.... Many theologians who have at their disposal only second-hand information run the risk of misunderstandings that are difficult to avoid. That very often does not prevent them from describing with great assurance events and discussions in which they did not take part. More than one inaccuracy (not to use other terms) has resulted from that—for example, in the conferences and publications of Fr. Schillebeeckx" (G. Philips, *L'Église et son mystère au deuxième Concile du Vatican*, vol. 2 [Tournai: Desclée, 1968], p. 307).

⚜

"[Some think] that the appended *Note* contains effectively a restriction of the text. For example, Cardinal Journet and Fr. Schillebeeckx. This latter opinion is without foundation", and so on. (As a note: E. Schillebeeckx, "Vaticanum II. 3e Sessie", *Kultuurleven* 32 [1965]: 21–38) (Philips, *L'Église*, vol. 1 [1967], pp. 283–84).

⚜

E. Schillebeeckx, in *Les Catholiques hollandais, rencontres et dialogues*, introduced by H. Hillenaar and H. Peters, trans. J. Alzin [Paris: DDB, 1969):

"The Church . . . has retreated into orthodoxy, finally abandoning orthopraxy to men who are outside the Church and to unbelievers" (p. 11).

"An atheistic interpretation [of life] has just as legitimate and rational a foundation as we have" (p. 12).

"Henceforward, the interpretation of the normative values of Scripture, of the tradition of the Church and of the Magisterium, will have a completely different look. So I would like to consider any affirmation of the Magisterium as a religious interpretation of salvation history at one given moment of that history. . . . The important thing is not the interpretation—each has his own—but to transform history together for the good of humanity" (pp. 13–14).

"Orthodoxy never sees the future, it only looks at the past" (p. 14).

"The hermeneutics of the Kingdom of God is above all to make the world better. . . . That is an element that passes from Marxism to the present time in theology" (p. 15).

"Any interpretation of man is pluralistic. . . . [We gave in the Church] an interpretation of reality on the basis of Christianity. Need we say that that time is past?" (pp. 17–18).

"Above everything else, I therefore wish for an absolute freedom for theologians, for they all want to be faithful to the Gospel" (p. 21).

"It is necessary that both the authentic, official Magisterium and the scholarly or theological magisterium, situated on a wholly different level, function in unison" (p. 22).

[Our journals] "are experiencing a new blossoming, now that the last vestiges of neo-Scholasticism have disappeared from their pages" (p. 20).

⚜

H. Oosterhuis (in *Les Catholiques hollandais*):

"There is no reason to define the liturgy as a service to render homage, as worship of God; in the first instance, the liturgy is presented on the level where all 'artistic' expression unfolds: theatre, song, cabaret. The differentiation is revealed afterward, in the reaction produced in men. . . . The liturgy is commonly presented as one form of expression and communication among all sorts of other forms" (p. 87).

[We must] "find an occasion to contest these words [of the Psalms], . . . to take them as the subject for dialogue or polemics. . . . It seems to me essential . . . to give substance to this confrontation of past and present, to implement this kind of connection between the trail traced from Israel up to our time and our own research" (pp. 88–89).

"In our liturgy . . . , it is the community that administers 'word and sacrament', and the priest merely carries out one function in this administration" (p. 97).

"The general style of the office must not be sacral" (pp. 97–98).

"Liturgy transcends the political insofar as it attains the level of artistic expression" (p. 103).

"In a feudal period of great patriarchal ownership, the emergence of a Church that took on the appearance of 'great ownership *of truth*', in which only the monologue was in current use, is not in the least surprising if considered from a sociological point of view. In rudimentary outline, we could see in this phenomenon the basic attitude of the Christian Churches since the Constantinian period" (E. Schillebeeckx, "L'Unique Témoignage et le dialogue dans la rencontre avec le monde", in *Oecumenica* [Paris-Neufchâtel, 1969], p. 1710).

"Rome's function is not to intervene in order to tell some particular local church that it must slow down and align itself with others. On the contrary, Rome can note the progress of one province of the Church and make it a stimulus for other provinces that are developing more slowly.... The central authority always remains, but its function is that of service: it is part of a synodal and democratic structure that, at the same time, is a specific structure of the Church...

"As authentic democratic structures begin to function in a single province of the Church, the idea will pass nearly automatically into others.... The formula, for example, adopted in Holland..." (E. Schillebeeckx, in *Sept problèmes capitaux de l'Église* [Paris: Fayard, 1969], pp. 125–27).

"Even those who cite Father Daniélou's name the most often are unaware of the fact that, right after the Second World War, he revived the 'new theology' with an article in *Études*..., giving rise to a veritable abscess, first in his own country, then even in the universities of Rome and, finally, right at the heart of the Holy Office, a situation whose true consequences were resolved, however, only in 1950, with the encyclical *Humani Generis* of Pius XII.

"The fact that Father Daniélou was not included by Cardinal Ottaviani in the preparatory theological commission surprises no one. Ottaviani had already had to swallow other affronts (Fr. Congar and Fr. de L., to cite only two); more need not have been asked of him. They could not have made him resign.... Caught between the hammer (his secretary at the Inquisition) and the anvil (the French cardinals), Pope Roncalli devised a reasonable compromise: to accept the exclusion of Fr. Daniélou during the preparatory period, but to command his participation during the term of the Council proper" (Carlo Falconi, *Vu et entendu au Concile*, trans. Ciccione [Monaco: Éditions du Rocher, 1965], pp. 71–72).

"The *potestas tenebrarum* [power of darkness] has an incredible strength, which finds no obstacle more adverse or more invincible than the defenseless weakness of the spirit. And it prevails. Yes, it prevails. History is also made up of these unfortunate events. The history of the Church is wholly woven from them. The Passion of Christ continues. We grasp a strange law in this, repugnant to our eyes; it is necessarily so. But it is a salutary law. It was necessary for Christ to suffer. And that is still true: it is necessary for the Church to suffer. For her fidelity to Christ. For her authenticity. In order to renew her capacity to speak to the world and to save it. Martyrdom is one of her charisms" (Cardinal J. B. Montini, Address at the Mass celebrated for Cardinal Stepinac in the cathedral of Milan, February 13, 1960, quoted by the journal *L'Italia*, Milan).

Episcopal Conferences

R. Laurentin, *L'Enjeu du Concile, 3. Bilan de la deuxième session* (Paris: Seuil, 1964), pp. 138–40, 234, 283, 290:

"The schema's overly exclusive emphasis on *national*

conferences was corrected. That level is dangerous, for it runs the risk of politicization.... To start from an a priori framework would also run the risk of forging new bureaucratic entities, all the more autocratic as they would be more abstract" (p. 140).

"The French were generally for a strict legislative power of territorial assemblies. Cardinal Frings, in the name of the German episcopal conference, came down against it: The Fulda conference has existed since 1847, he explained. The statutes do not have juridical force; they have nonetheless had good effects. Each bishop governs his diocese according to his conscience, but there is mutual aid that opens out into international mutual aid.... May the schema not therefore urge the establishment of provincial councils or the founding of a permanent secretariat. There is a danger in that. May there be a reduction in the number of cases where the decisions of the conference are imposed. May a four-fifths vote be required to that effect. Let us respect ... the freedom of each and charity toward all" (p. 138).

"'Those who defended the personal powers of the bishops feared that the latter would be stifled by a dominant collectivism" (p. 139).

"What is irreversible is the restoration of an organic collegial awareness, which is due to the very constitution of the hierarchy founded by Christ and more profoundly to the importance of the values of communion in the Church.... What is irreversible, correlatively, is the necessity of this new awareness within the framework of a world in the process of increasing socialization and internationalization" (p. 234).

Ordo episcoporum: Tertullian.
Corpus, collegium . . . : Cyprian.
Collegium episcoporum: Optatus of Milevia.
Corpus episcoporum: Gasser at Vatican I (p. 283).

Bishop Bontems regrets that the Germans did not follow the French in asking for obligatory force of law for the decisions of the conferences (cf. *La Documentation catholique*, December 15, 1963, no. 1414, co. 1671, quoted in R. Laurentin, *L'Enjeu*, p. 290).

René Laurentin, *L'Enjeu*, pp. 52–53, 153:

"One must recall, too, the peripheral vitality of the Council. . . . How many public and private meetings . . . , working lunches and dinners, oriented at first toward the Council and then, increasingly, toward the "postconciliar" . . . ! Never had so many conferences been organized. . . . Then there was the crowd of journalists. . . . Out of their meetings came the project of a postconciliar center for religious information" (p. 52, "La Vitalité conciliaire et paraconciliaire"). "Disseminators of all kinds of ideas could be seen passing by . . ." (p. 53).

"Why is the press familiar with only five or six theologians and completely silent about other names?" (153).

⚜

On Collegiality

"This given of faith has been obscured in recent times" (p. 52).

"Few theological theses can be established so easily, so fully" (p. 53).

"Collegiality by divine right and even universal collegial jurisdiction are not anything recent. It is a traditional thesis . . . , attested to with particular clarity [by] the champions of papal infallibility, from Christianopoulos to Bolgeni, and to Cappellari . . ." (p. 54).

"Collegiality is therefore, in short, transparently obvious, rather like the air we breathe" (ibid.).

⚜

Excerpts from J. Lortz, *La Réforme de Luther*, vol. 1, trans. D. Olivier (Paris: Cerf, 1970):

"All that is needed at present to reveal the inadequate influence of the traditional faith over consciences is to bring out the weak points, by means of a more intense criticism, and to offer some radically simplifying novelties" (p. 37).

"Any serious weakening of the Church opens the way to a *radical* criticism and to its success" (p. 46).

"The danger was also in the fullness of the movement . . . that brought the people of the Church to have more contact with the times, for love of the world annihilated in them any will to maintain the transcendence of the sacred or to defend the absolute character of the Christian demands against the accommodation of the humanist morality" (p. 123).

"Having lost sight of the profound reality of the priesthood, they had been reduced to a clericalism that retained no more than the most external, the most secularized aspects of it" (p. 135).

"By means of a secret contagion, all the events, from that moment [1519] on, took on an importance that went beyond the intentions of the actors" (p. 309).

"[The bishops] were [at that time] everything, except leaders. From the beginning, their silence and their inertia made them the ones primarily responsible for the turn taken by events. Their behavior with regard to the bull *Exsurge Domine* is sufficient proof of this" (pp. 360–61).

"The ease with which the most sacred bonds were broken made the reforming fever rise, and it began to give a dramatic turn to the process of laicization" (p. 423).

"The anabaptists . . . applied literally the Lutheran precept of the conformity of all life with the word of God, so that there was no longer any secular life for them: even economic and social life had to be ruled directly by the Gospel" (p. 431).

"The enthusiasts embody the ever-recurring tendency in the Church to live Christianity in small communities guided solely by the Spirit, apart from the mass of Christians and without any ties to the hierarchy or to dogma" (p. 432).

"Right at the dawn of the Reformation, the biblical principle and the spiritualism of faith manifest the disastrous ferment of decay that Luther's unilateral ideas carry with them" (p. 439).

"The ones largely to blame are the bishops.... These bishops ... were generally ignorant, ineffective leaders" (p. 477).

"Luther liked to recall that many bishops had begun by looking favorably on his assaults against papal power" (p. 478).

"The inertia of many bishops.... *They can at least be reproached for never having been able to make the essential decisions at the proper moment*" (p. 479, emphasis in the text).

"Everyone [in Germany] seems to be losing heart, but that stimulates me all the more. The Catholic princes and the bishops do not know what to do; they tolerate married priests, preachers who are half-Lutheran.... There is not a Catholic who does not read heretical works; in fact those are the only ones being sold" (Jérôme Nadal to Ignatius of Loyola, Vienna, May 8, 1555, in *Epistolae Nadal*, vol. 1, Monumenta historica S. J. [1898], pp. 301–2).

"A sociologist studying the phenomenon of the rapid and vast response encountered by *Humanae vitae*

would no doubt stress the power of the influence exercised by the *mass media*. The latter, in scarcely twenty-four hours, succeeded, with the help of slogans and phrases chosen for their shock value, in marking public opinion in such a way that reading the whole document came, in many minds, as a superimposition over a first judgment already imposed, a judgment that was no stranger to either passion or myth. Increasingly, the active role of this power that 'information' represents will be a determining factor in modern society. This fact, over which there is little control, does not fail to carry with it some weighty consequences for the spread of the Church's message" (Georges Cottier, *Régulation des naissances et développement démographique* [Paris: DDB, 1969], p. 7).

"Everywhere, for the past dozen years or so, we see the same absurd scheme, the same black-and-white contrast of a chronological Manichaeism: 'Yesterday', everything was black (this 'yesterday' being labeled at will as the capitalist era, or post-Tridentine, or feudal, or medieval, or Constantinian, or postapostolic, or even at times apostolic, as if they were the same thing; all was in error, mythical, illusory, idiotic, infantile, hypocritical, static, oppressive, and so forth: take your pick). Today, everything is white, or at least is going to be white tomorrow: all we need, for the complete implementation of the miracle that has begun, is to be 'in the wind', to silence the 'traditionalists', to invoke the spirit of the Council or its 'dynamics', to understand that it has 'opened a breach' without being concerned about its content, to contest everything of the 'preconciliar Church', to be a part of the 'new Church', to call any dissolution, any abandonment, 'progress'; to celebrate everything blindly as a conquest of 'criticism'. That way we maintain a good conscience of the best triumphalist style. This cliché could not be avoided even in the context of a eucharistic congress (Bogota, 1968). A Benedictine proclaimed there: 'Before the Second Vatican Council, to practice Catholicism was to adhere to an institution; now, it is to be integrated into a community. Formerly, one made the Church the Kingdom of God already achieved; now we have understood that it is a question of a progress toward the Kingdom'" (T. M.; cf. *La Croix*, August 21, 1968, p. 3). Again, that is only one small example.

"He recounted to me a system of the priesthood completely identical with an organization of urban guards. The priest would be taken indiscriminately and temporarily from all classes of society: without past and without future, without divine mission and without sacred character, this improvised priest would leave his bench, his counter, even his workshop, in order to do his guard duty beside our soul; he would be relieved by a companion like a guard coming off duty" (Mme. Cottu, on her conversation with Lamennais in 1840; in

P. Dudon, *Lamennais et le Saint-Siège 1820–1834,* 2d. ed [Paris: Perrin et Cie, 1911], p. 367; cf. *Lettres inédites de Lamennais à la baronne Cottu*, published by the Comte d'Houssonville [Paris: Éditions Perrin Histoire, 1910], p. 45).

III

Mysteries, Doctrine, Tradition, Faith

I learned in my little catechism, more than seventy years ago, that the Christian religion contains three great mysteries: the mystery of the Trinity, the mystery of the Incarnation, and the mystery of the Redemption. Since then, I have had occasion to read a lot and to hear a lot; I have seen many doctrines proposed and compared. I have never found anything that enlightens human existence as well, that opens up more immense avenues for human reflection, that penetrates as profoundly the mystery that is man himself. All the social evolutions and revolutions, all the scientific progress, all the views of the future change nothing. That, I realize, is not immediately apparent. Some might think that the formulas that encompass these three mysteries, too abstract to grip the understanding of a child, are equally so for the spiritual nourishment of an adult. A first act of trust is therefore indispensable. The child's understanding, if it is awakened in a seriously Catholic environment, in which faith is the source of life, produces this spontaneously. The adult must verify the grounds for his belief. The latter come to him from a Church that calls herself his Mother. What are the grounds for this Church? He could content himself with contemplating her history, and already this would be legitimate: if one reflects on it even a little, nothing is more admirable, more worthy of belief than the permanence and the development of this institution across the centuries—whatever might be all the human weaknesses observed in her, which is all many petty minds, claiming to be clairvoyant critics, wish to see in her: precisely the practiced eye discerns in her what is not of man; in the history of the Church, he reads, even if at times beneath the surface, the history of sanctity. One can subsequently, however, if need be, seek to verify more rigorously the claims of this Church by referring to her origins. Now it is manifestly clear that she was not at first a gathering of people, the result of a free association of believers, sharing a common ideal conceived by them in order to live it. Such an association would not have lasted very long, and, moreover, the best attested history, which generations of critical studies have only brought out more clearly in its essential traits, shows us something quite different. The Church is the work of Jesus (the call of the "Twelve") and of his Spirit. If, after having glimpsed the depths in which they make us penetrate, one still finds the three great mysteries that this Church teaches us "too good to be true", and if one remarks as well that their conceptual formulation (which is very incomplete, moreover), with all the scholarly details that have been added to it, becomes a puzzle for the modern intelligence and that it did not exist in the beginning, one can in all conscience escape the scruple born of this twofold observation. The first, which presupposes a knowledge of the technicalities of philosophical language and of its evolution, carries with it its own remedy, for it is the attribute of the educated man, whatever certain sophists say, to recognize himself across the diversities and transformation of cultures and to further the continuation of what is human there. As for the second remark, it will be granted merely by observing that, under a more concrete form, which will never be "transcended", the faith of the early Church already contained the perfectly explicit belief in each of these three mysteries: one need only read the texts of the New Testament, the first attested baptismal formulas, the first creeds of the faith. One can even narrow the focus more by seeing that the very teaching of Jesus, as discreet as it may have been, about his work and his person, presupposes or leads to this threefold mystery.

How do we dare continue to live, simply, prosaically, even virtuously, with the thousand small advantages, whether sought or not, accepted in any case, of everyday existence, even during dark times and under the weight of insurmountable trials—and how can we still welcome in good conscience even the most humble, most meager joys that blossom at times along the way—when we have seriously considered the abyss in which Jesus was engulfed, when the ear of our heart has truly registered the final cry of his distress? How is it that the sight offered every day of the continued suffering today in his Church, which is his Body, torn, misunderstood, held up to ridicule by her own members, does not awaken the need to unite ourselves to so much distress, or the shame of neglecting to do so every day?

That learned theologian, a highly skilled professor, who finds no teaching on prayer in the Psalms . . .

Those learned exegetes, highly skilled critics, who find nothing about the ministerial priesthood in the New Testament or in Ignatius of Antioch, nothing "sacred" in the first Christian century . . .

Those learned historians of the Church who find nothing about episcopal collegiality in the first centuries, nor anything on the papacy . . .

They need words, abstractions, definitions, theses; they need theology manuals and a *Codex juris canonici* written by the twelve apostles in a "workshop", in the Cenacle.

"In general," Heinrich Schlier observes, "conceptual precision is not given at the origin of a thing but belongs to its later development" (*Le Temps de l'Église*, trans. François Corin [Tournai: Casterman, 1961], p.

264). And this law is especially well verified when the thing in question has deep roots.

In order for Jesus of Nazareth to be revealed to us as the Christ, truly worthy of faith, they want him to be presented to us by "objective" historians who leave us free to judge for ourselves. In other words, the vision given us by these historians must owe nothing to their faith; they must have no other connection with him than that of a certain historical curiosity. Only this should have impelled them to write. If Jesus has turned something upside down within their being, then their account becomes a testimony, and for that very reason it is suspect. From the moment they believe in him, they can no longer speak of him with that impartial detachment that alone could eventually arouse our own faith.

Nothing could be more absurd. This would mean that historical testimony and testimony of faith would be contradictory; that the latter would weaken the former. If the witnesses to Jesus believed in him, this would supposedly be precisely the reason that would prevent us from believing in him; at least, from believing what they tell us. In order for us to be able to believe in Jesus on their word, it would be necessary that they themselves not have believed in him, or at least that their language kept their own faith hidden from us.

⚜

Theological charlatanism. Because Charles Davis leaves the Church, marries, and spares no effort on television in a rather petty campaign against the Church, Hans Küng salutes him as "the most renowned Catholic theologian in England"; he lines up all the titles he can find, including, of course, "member of the directorial committee of the international theological journal *Concilium*", and crowns him "pillar of the movement for ecclesial renewal in England". Even more, he says his departure from the Church "has a general significance. Quite like the movement in the opposite direction by another English theologian of the last century: John Henry Newman." Küng draws from this "an appeal to the Church". Not content with having written that in an article announcing the event, at the beginning of 1967, he reproduces it in his book *Être vrai: L'Avenir de l'Église* (French trans. H. Rochais [Paris: DDB, 1968], pp. 65–66), in which those who know the truth of the matter would not have difficulty discerning, besides the unjust excesses, some hypocrisy.

All that is absolutely charlatanism. But, by means of mass publicity, all over the world this is all thrust upon young priests, seminarians, religious, and so forth, who have no means of verifying it. And here, shortly after, we have in *La Croix*, from the pen of an Assumptionist, Charles Davis becoming the greatest English-language theologian of our time. Of course, in this concert of praise, the name of no other English theologian, Catholic, Anglican, Presbyterian or otherwise, is cited; and yet one would be very hard-pressed to discover the least citation of this Davis put forward as an authority by any serious work of theology in any language. Soon, however, a sensationalist journalist . . . writes a preface for a new book by Davis, whom he, too, presents as "the greatest English theologian", and he wants to make us believe that, because he had accompanied his bishop to Rome for the Council, this banal fact has sufficed to consecrate Davis in the eyes of the whole universe as a great theologian . . .[1]

It is in this way that the Church is poisoned.

Poor great Newman, whose name they dare to mingle with such stupidity . . .

I have read, in a Christian journal, something ridiculing one of the articles of the *Credo*: "He is seated at the right hand of". And this kind of mockery, which at times affects a grave tone or an expression of pity for the mental deficients who were our fathers in the faith, is increasingly common these days. It is rather to us, under the influence of Voltaire, that the mockery should be addressed—or the pity. As for discussing it seriously, that would be doing it too much honor. The testimony of the Christian tradition is enough. We have always known that the images were

[1] And the publicity flyer of an American publisher did not hesitate to present Küng and his group as new Thomas Aquinases, "the greatest architects of the postconciliar Church. . . ."

images, and we have always known how to translate them—while rightly preferring to preserve expressions full of imagery, always so pregnant with a truth that is richer than their translation. Commenting on the Book of Job, which speaks to us of a dialogue between God and Satan, Luis de Leon explains to us: "And all that, which never actually happened as it is represented in the imagination of the prophet, did actually happen in accordance with what that image signifies." And this is not a belated Christian allegorism: "No Jew would ever have imagined that certain of these [biblical] metaphors could be taken literally" (G. L. Prestige, *God in Patristic Thought* [London: SPCK, 1956], p. 8).

In order to dare proclaim everything that appeared in the past to be part of a superseded [*depassée*] culture, one must either always look only at mediocre things or else—through a penchant for systematizing or through congenital mediocrity—reduce in advance everything that is sublime and profound to the mediocre.

It is the characteristic of great things always to "transcend" [*dépasser*] the bounds of the particular "culture" in which they were engendered.

It is possible to caricature everything: morality, mysticism, obedience, faith, religion, tradition, piety, and so forth. And some do not abstain from doing so. One whole part of our "religious" literature, and a part that becomes more intrusive every day, is made up of these caricatures, through the Manichaean play of antitheses, one of whose terms serves to repel the other.

The very simple religion of my mother: how much more truth it had, how much more vital substance, than that of these doctors and professors, so pretentious, so disdainful—and how much more than mine.

A certain Orthodox theologian, in the introduction to one of his books, exhorts his reader to enter thoroughly into the perspective of Orthodoxy—and he finds a large audience. A certain Catholic theologian strives, from one end of his book to the other, to enter into the perspective of the non-Catholic, indeed, of the unbeliever, thinking thereby to make himself "credible"—and he finds no audience at all—if, in his desire for adaptation, he has not resorted to dropping a part of the Catholic *Credo* altogether. These are not exceptional cases on either side. A person can be both humble and proud of his faith at the same time. Whether he is humble or not, if he is ashamed of his faith, it is better to keep silent. Should this contrast between the two attitudes not in any case lead us to reflect about our present conceptions of adaptation, of openness, and of dialogue, which, perhaps, have something distorted about them? But is it not in reality a question of a more fundamental evil?

"Paris", Péguy said in 1907, "is full of people who always know how to write something new and to say something different. Let us admire these people of Paris" (*Oeuvres en prose*, vol. 1, Bibliothèque de la Pléiade [Paris: Gallimard, 1959], p. 1125).

Among these people of Paris, a crowd of scholars holds a place of honor. Some of them conspired in 1975 to launch a new journal whose very title is a masterpiece: *Autrement* [Differently].

But like the good Homer of old, they are sometimes apt to nod off. The impetus flags, invention gives way to routine. The second issue of the journal was still called *Autrement*.

Infallibility. Some theologians reject the word, as applied to the definitions enunciated by the pope, and along with the word they reject the thing itself. Of course, it is necessary to understand this notion within the limitations and with the precautions noted by Vatican I itself; of course, too, it is necessary to understand it within the general notion of truth, which a philosophy of the human understanding and a theology of divine revelation would always have to examine thoroughly. But the thing itself is to be firmly retained. Some, however, while retaining the thing, would be ready to sacrifice the word. The spirit of conciliation that prompts them to do this is laudable. Nevertheless, I cannot follow them. The words they propose as substitutions are not felicitous. On the other hand, we know that the councils have often been constrained to have recourse to unscriptural terms (ever since the "consubstantial" of Nicaea) in order to protect and define the faith more accurately; whereas here the very word happens to be scriptural: "I have prayed that your faith may not fail" [Lk 22:32].

Dedicated to our clerics who weaken the very idea of dogma with their sarcasm:

"Many a man will live and die upon a dogma: no man will be a martyr for a conclusion.... No one, I say, will die for his own calculations: he dies for realities" (Newman, *Grammar of Assent* [Notre Dame, Ind., and London: Univ. of Notre Dame Press, 1979], p. 89).

Dedicated to those who see in the dogma of the Trinity only an uninteresting abstraction:

"Let us embrace the sacred Mystery of the Trinity in Unity, which, as the Creed tells us, is the ground of the Catholic religion. Let us think it enough, let us think it far too great a privilege, for sinners such as we are, for a fallen people in a degenerate age, to inherit the faith once delivered to the Saints; let us accept it thankfully; let us guard it watchfully; let us transmit it faithfully to those who come after us" (Newman, "Faith without Demonstration", sermon 23, in *Parochial and Plain Sermons* [San Francisco: Ignatius Press, 1987], p. 1388).

They thunder against all "apologetics"—and they never stop seeking to make Christianity "credible" *by detached pieces*—which is the worst of apologetics.

The desire for rupture is exalted today as the impossibility of communication.

Only the absence of culture makes the various cultures impermeable to each other.

When the Spirit withdraws, theology becomes a "critical function", and the priestly ministry, a "profession".

Has Monsieur Homais, in his old age, been converted to adult Christianity, or have our Christian adults, in their juvenile fervor, become Monsieur Homais?[2]

Discreet faith: Yes.—Shamefaced faith: No.

They speak only of creativity. And they are gripped by an insane negativity. Criticism without love, violence, demolition, self-destruction.

There are many ways, all equally pernicious, of giving in to an inflation of the idea of culture. In reaction against an abstract, simplistic, and superficial universalism, a whole pluralism is established today, through division and compartmentalization, of what is called "the cultures", and by doing so they end up ruining all human culture.

"Intolerance is the first sign of an inadequate education. An ill-educated person behaves with arrogant

---

[2] Monsieur Homais is a character seen as the embodiment of petit-bourgeois stupidity in Gustave Flaubert's novel *Madame Bovary*.—TRANS.

impatience, whereas truly profound education breeds humility" (Alexander Solzhenitsyn, *August 1914*, trans. Michael Glenny [New York: Farrar, Straus and Giroux, 1971], p. 409; Varsonofiev addressing the two students Kotya and Sanya).

Plurality is a fact, pluralism is a system—one that has been exalted as an ideal. The former is observed; the latter is asserted. The movement of faith tends to rise above plurality, through a spontaneous convergence, while pluralism, through the conscious desire for differentiation, affects faith itself.

The Enlightenment "would have regarded the conception of 'two cultures' as the equivalent to no culture at all" (Norman Hampson, *A Cultural History of the Enlightenment* [New York: Pantheon Books, 1968], p. 11). Today, however, some give the Enlightenment as a reference while preaching the pluralism of cultures.

One theologian tells us that our West, having arrived at the evening of its life, must rethink with its present philosophy the message of the Gospel. He judges that this would be doing today what the Fathers of the

Church and then the theologians of the Middle Ages did in their time.

I would say rather that the believing philosopher must strive today to rethink the philosophy of the West according to the messages of the Gospel. This reverse formula seems to me to correspond better to what the Fathers of the Church and the medievals did in their time. The two cases, in whatever way their relationship is considered, cannot be identical, moreover, for one cannot disregard that great, massive fact: the ancient philosophies, whether in the time of the Fathers or in that of a Saint Thomas, were not at all in the same relationship to the Christian faith as are the current philosophies of our West.

The person "can give himself, *as a person*, only insofar as he remains consciously united with himself, that is to say, *distinct*" (P. Teilhard de Chardin, *Esquisse d'un Univers personnel*, in *Oeuvres*, vol. 6, *L'Énergie humaine* [Paris: Seuil, 1962], p. 84).

So it is with the Church today, with respect to the world. She must be ever more open to the world in order to give herself to it, which is to say, in order to communicate to it the Spirit of Christ which has been given to her and who lives in her.

The temptation to let oneself go instead of giving oneself: that is the temptation of our time.

⚜

... So many professors, well settled in their chairs, surrounded by their assistants and their secretaries, strutting around in congresses, who dream of retirement and honorary memberships, who expect or solicit flattering reviews of their works—and who always have on their lips "decisive" sentences, words of "total faith" that are more assuredly pure, more demanding, more severe, more exposed, more radical, than the poor objectified, superstitious, reassuring faith of the Church and so on . . .

So many "existentialists" who are so little alive [*existant*] . . .

If by chance they see a man of God, they are unable to recognize him. They fabricate for themselves inferior substitutes, which they adore as idols, and by means of which they secretly adore themselves.

In the expression "secularized world", wielded like a slogan, taken to be a primary truth, everything is mixed together: the cosmos, culture, society, even the Church. They declare the process irreversible, without taking into account all the resacralizing, which is often miserable and at times terribly deadly. It is linked to "pluralism", another slogan that lends itself to a hundred different interpretations, and these two expressions—by which they claim to sum up, with the objectivity of a sociologist, two great connected facts—are in reality placed more or less implicitly at the service of an ideal. Then, under their cover, a new intransigent sacred, a new intolerant dogmatism is set up in the same minds.

Appeal is made to the Creator God taught by the Bible in order to profane, desacralize, secularize the world—then all faith in God is suppressed in the name of a profaned, desacralized, secularized world.

The world is desacralized in the name of transcendence—then pure immanence is proclaimed in the name of this desacralized world.

They preach to us a Christianity "without myth", and that would be perfect if they did not confuse myth with any symbolic expression at all. The "ultimate realities", the "mysteries of the faith" are accessible to us only in an envelope of symbols. It is the nature of rationalism to claim to translate the symbol into concepts and thereby to destroy the truth given in the symbol.

"God is given essentially to man *as* sacred mystery. . . . He would not be God if he ceased to be this sacred mystery" (K. Rahner, *Le Concept de mystère dans la théologie catholique*, trans. R. Givord, in *Écrits théologiques* [Paris: DDB] 8:78).

Whatever Victor Cousin says, there are more things in "the half-light of symbols" than in "the full light of pure thought", and if, as Kant said, "the symbol gives much to thought", thought does not exhaust the symbol. A philosopher is either very pretentious or very naïve if he believes he has gone beyond the region of symbols, as a plane rises into the skies above the level of clouds.

The "stop-gap god", the "consoler god", the "refuge god", the "emperor god of the world"—there we have four of those "old idols" that every day a new prophet invites us to destroy in order finally to make room for the true God.

How could anyone disagree? But they should perhaps begin by telling us that these are four caricatures, or four distortions—to which in one way or another man is exposed at all times—of four great truths, instead of wanting to convince us that this was until yesterday the faith of the Church and that it must be changed.

Where, then, either in the professions of faith or in the treatises of "natural theology", or in the spiritual tradition of the Christian centuries, do we find, for example, this concept of a "stop-gap god"? Nowhere. That is because, first of all, and for solid reasons, they believed in God, and, with an imperfect knowledge of nature, they could attribute to his miraculous intervention certain extraordinary natural facts.

⚜

"A ravenous activism among Christians and clergy, a certain generalized, rationalistic coldness of heart, an atrophied sense of contemplation and mysticism, a lack of prayerful theology, the temptation to want to expect the whole salvation of the Church from purely institutional changes": such were the disturbing signs that Fr. Karl Rahner discerned, in June 1966, several months after the end of the Council (cf. *Serviteurs du Christ*, trans. Muller [Tours: Mame, 1969], p. 131). It would be interesting to take a reading ten years later. Karl Rahner reckoned that others would not share his opinion, but he hoped that, with the grace of the Holy Spirit, these disturbing signs would not last. Is it any different today?

The Church is threatened today, wrote Pastor André Dumas, "not by religious or clerical omnipotence, but by marginalism, insignificance, and evanescence" *(Une théologie de la réalité: Dietrich Bonhœffer* [Geneva: Labor et Fides, 1968], p. 279).

This diagnosis, made several years ago, was just as valid for Catholicism. But since then, "insignificance and evanescence" have no longer remained a marginal phenomenon. They have—at least in part—conquered those in power. This insignificance and this evanescence of the new faith preached by those who were at that time "dissidents" are maintained, taught, and imposed by them. The great danger today is the clerical omnipotence of an insignificant and evanescent Christianity.

No Stone Unturned

In the name of the people of God, who know no boundaries, as in the name of the little elite advance posts of the Diaspora. In the name of implicit Christianity and of the treasures of salvation objectively contained in all religion, as in the name of a pure, a-religious Christianity. In the name of a free Christianity, without laws, without dogmas, without authority, open to all the winds of the Spirit, as in the name of new, solidly forged structures. In the name of a pure faith marvelously detached from all cultural events, as in the name of a new culture that takes the place of faith. In the name of an exaggerated personalism that destroys any idea of nature in relation to the idea of creation as in the name of the "human sciences" that some want, destructive of all free personality. In the name of a prophetism confirming all individual fantasies, as in the name of a sociologism that stifles all initiatives of the Spirit in the Church. In the name of a Russian type of Marxism, as in the name of an anarchism excommunicated by the Party. In the name of a distant past of which some trait or other is exalted, as in the name of a mature present and of a bewitching future that can no longer tolerate the past. In the name of critical science, as in the name of a pastoral letter to the most humble. In the name of a critic of rationalism as in the name of a critic of fideism, and so on. It is of little importance that these are so many contradictory bases, as long as they serve as fortresses or trenches from which to launch an assault against the Church and the faith that she upholds for us.

They leave no stone unturned.

No Stone Unturned (continued)

I read in a doctrinal program: "It is necessary to banish all apologetics"—and, a few lines farther on: "It is necessary to make the sacraments credible."

Read also this astonishing phrase: "It is necessary to lead the Church back to her origins, to the pre-Constantinian age", which is to say, "to the era of the great councils".

Read a panegyric of the Enlightenment, which is par excellence the century of superficial rationalism and the century of the idea of nature—and, in the same setting, read and heard many a diatribe against the "rationalism" of traditional philosophy and against the idea of nature, which made the documents of the hierarchy unacceptable.

The "hellenization" of Christianity is bitterly deplored, and the first Canon of the Mass is set aside, the only canon that is of ancient Semitic structure, in favor of the others, which bear the mark of later "hellenism".

The most obvious contradictions do not matter as long as they serve to criticize the Church, her dogma, her teachings, her morality, her liturgy. They leave no stone unturned.

The same ones preach a return to Luther and want the Christian to live his faith in insecurity. They do not know that Luther said "Christianum oportet semper securum esse [the Christian ought always to be secure]" (1518; cf. L. Febvre, *Un destin, Martin Luther* [Paris: Éd. Predes, 1928], pp. 67–68).

"When the Church has made dogmatic formulations about Jesus' person using terms that were not all taken literally from Scripture, she did so only in order to defend the attestation of the Spirit against dialecticians who, incapable of grasping the unity of it, reconstructed on their own level of intelligence a mystery in itself too untenable" (Paul Toinet, *La Foi sur la terre* [1969], c. 5).

It is easy to caricature the idea of the divine transcendence by saying that it "adds to the world a fantastic doublet", or the idea of eternal life by saying that it adds to this temporal life the extension of another indefinitely continued life. This is getting out of it a bit too lightly.

⚜

"This disparagement of doctrinal statements, and in particular of those relating to the Holy Trinity and Incarnation, is especially prevalent in our times. There is a suspicion widely abroad . . . that the development of ideas and formation of dogmas is a mere abuse of Reason. . . . It is my purpose, then, . . . to investigate the connexion between Faith and Dogmatic Confession" (John Henry Newman, *Newman's University Sermons: Fifteen Sermons Preached before the University of Oxford 1826–43* [London: SPCK, 1970], fifteenth sermon, nos. 8–9).

⚜

"The last [of my University Sermons], which I preached, on the 'Purification', lasted an hour and a half! People went about saying there was a good deal of mischief in it, and that it must be answered; but I am under no apprehensions. And so, you see, I am altogether very tranquil" (John Henry Newman, Letter to his sister Jemina, February 21, 1843; *Letters and Correspondence of John Henry Newman during His Life in the English Church*, ed. Anne Mozley [London: Longmans, Green, 1903]).

⚜

"It is possible to affirm, with exact and precise proof in support of it, that the great theological and ecclesiastical catastrophe of which German Protestantism is currently the theater would not have been produced if the three words *Filium ejus unicum*, in the exact sense of the Nicene doctrine of the Trinity, had not in fact disappeared for the German Church for more than two centuries under a confused mass of interpretations that watered them down. In . . . other countries . . . , they would do well to consider this catastrophe as a warning" (Karl Barth, *Credo*, trans. P. and J. Jundt [Paris, 1936], p. 67).

That should make us reflect on the abandonment, in the Creed, of "consubstantial".

"I pray that you have the strength to fight and help us get out of this tragedy into which our clergy and religious have sunk. Let them understand that they are going to provoke reactions. *We will not follow them*."—The "we" here are men who have suffered tragically from integrism.—"This powerful neo-modernism is without true intellectual concern. With some, there is real generosity and naïve adolescence. But I fear these priests who no longer have faith, who remain in the Church with the intention of leading other priests astray and of perverting the laity. Their sole ideal is a vague progressivism. . . . Some make reference to Loisy in private, but they have not felt his tragedy, which cannot be theirs.—I do not agree with the 'manifesto' issued by the theologians,[3] in

---

[3] This was a manifesto issued by the journal *Concilium* in 1968.

which it pained me to find the name of X. Of course, under Pius XII, I would have understood such a text. But in 1968, in the present debacle, it seems to me a serious infidelity to the Spirit. Our priests are troubled, very troubled, by it; they are at times in the most appalling anguish; all they have loved is kicked out: self-destruction, the end of Christianity. . . .

"—The theology they give *themselves* expresses a personal or collective unconscious, toward which they tend obscurely. . . . Everything is abandoned by the theologians, religious—even by Jesuits, Father. . . . When a priest tells me that Christianity is only the tradition of a myth, he does not see that he has lost the secret of the Christian soul, which used to speak of Mystery. . . . Our faith can only be that of the praying Church, pure, holy, without stain. Many modern, so-called Catholic theologians no longer understand this."

. . . Is there really nothing for you any more in the heart of man that has a value in and of itself? Are you not happy if one day you happen to catch a glimpse of a pure heart? Do you ask right away, with cold calculation, "What is the good of that?" Do you never suffer when faced with evidence of a base sensibility, even if you are in no way touched by it? Is it not painful for you to find a soul closing itself to any religious impulse? In the depths of yourself, are you quietly content with having banished even the word *soul*?

Because I do not curse all apologetics and because I speak, along with those who instructed me in the faith, of my "reasons for believing", I am reproached by one person for my naturalism. And, because I do not set myself above my faith—above my Lord!—I am reproached by another for my fideism. The one would like a wholly irrational faith; the other accepts only a faith fully "understood". The one would like to hear me say, without even making any distinctions: *Credo quia absurdum*;[4] the other requires me to "understand" my faith completely—which would no longer be my faith. It may be that both the one and the other are, in the depths of themselves, true disciples of the Lord (the human heart is unfathomable). As for me, I try to put myself in a position that makes it intelligible to be one.

Every time I let myself be impressed by the surface appearance—and I do not say by its vanity but by its terrible seriousness—I am tempted by incredulity.

---

[4] "I believe because it is absurd", a quotation from Tertullian, *De Carne Christi* 5, in response to the question how he could believe in a God who allowed himself to suffer the supreme humiliation of the Cross.—Trans.

Every time reflection regains the upper hand, it again opens to me the way that leads in the direction of faith. Faith always remains difficult—but incredulity proves to be impossible. It is not a fear of pessimism and despair; it is not the attraction of consolation or at least of security that propels me back to faith. It is the (always pale) victory of the spirit over carnal sensibility.

But what introduces and sustains in faith is of a different order.

I have heard it said around me that faith is becoming difficult, that objections of all kinds arise the moment one begins to reflect. My own experience is the opposite. When I grow weary of reflection, when I drag along the surface of myself, when I no longer have the strength to think or the taste for prayer, that is when the temptation "not to believe in anything anymore" insinuates itself in vagueness and the most banal imprecision. The whole depth of reality grows blurred, everything seems "problematic", because no problem is dealt with seriously. It is life according to appearances—without even that barren depth of a theory—however inconsistent—of the absurd. It is just the opposite of a critical flash piercing the clouds. It is a hazy state and a dullness from which I have to shake myself. And it is then in that sense, and in only that sense, that I can say that faith is difficult for me.

Some of our contemporaries who still sincerely refer to Christianity and do not wish to break with the Church freely call any doctrine "ideology" that they have not first discovered themselves, as the fruit of their personal experience. Only the latter would be the bearer (indeed, creator) of true Christianity. They thus set a narrow, uprooted experience against the vast, profound experience inherited from the first apostles of Christ and preserved, protected, and thoroughly examined by generations of Christians under the guarantee of the Church's ministry. They no longer want the objectivity of Mystery, the sole principle of a truly Christian experience, but make each of their individual experiences an absolute. This mysticism without mystery, if it does not dissolve into insignificance, can be the source of multiple aberrations. Fortunately, those who insist on it still participate, without perceiving it, in that Mystery which they call ideology, and the traces of this objective Mystery, preserved for all in the dogmatic formulas, are what still assure to their experience a remnant of Christian value. How much more realistic, however, and how much more substantial in their spiritual action, are those who, less concerned about themselves, find in the Mystery of the Holy Trinity exactly what the Church proposes to them in her formulas, the ever and endlessly fruitful, infinitely transcendent, living principle of their own experience!

"One Church, one community, in which activity is concentrated in the official ministers to the exclusion of other members would make one seriously question whether, in leaving the charisms 'dormant', one had not also voided the Spirit" (Hans Küng, "La Structure charismatique de l'Église", *Concilium* 4 [1965]: 56).

Absurd. At what time would or could all "activity" of the Church have been so concentrated? It has never been alleged that, besides the bishops and pope, there have not been saints or geniuses or writers or theologians or founders or devoted and resourceful Christians of all kinds, and so on. And this is said in the form of a threat at a time when the authority of the Church is held up to ridicule, which makes the absurd odious as well. And what does "charismatic structure" mean? Great and wicked words. What threatens us in a much more real way is a situation in which some "Professors" succeed in controlling, through the pressure tactics at their disposal today, a usurped authority that would sterilize the "activity" of the Church.

For positive science, there is (there can be) neither quality nor value; there is neither personal being nor even any synthesis that cannot be broken down. There is not (nor can there be) any genius, any heroes, any saint: those are things that cannot be measured or counted. The objective accuracy of a text can be strictly verified, but science can say nothing about the profundity or the pointlessness of a thought. For science, man is an object, who in no way "goes beyond man": such an affirmation would be absurd for it. It has something else to do, something very legitimate, very instructive, and often of great practical importance. But it is great naïveté on the part of the scholar, of the "seeker", to believe himself obliged to deny what he has systematically begun to disregard, what he does not find because he does not seek it and cannot find because he cannot seek it.

For positive science, there are no "transcendentals". The true, the beautiful, the good signify nothing for it. They are "of a different order". "Love unveils the soul that analytical curiosity destroys" (G. Picon, commenting on Bernanos, in *Bernanos, Oeuvres romanesques*, Bibliothèque de la Pléiade [Paris: Gallimard, 1961], p. XII).

"I have never seen Catholic Spain", wrote Malraux in *L'Espoir*. "I have seen some rituals and, in the soul as in the countryside, a desert." He was perspicacious, but undoubtedly he was not in a position to see well.

In Grenada, at the end of a little street that led down to the entrance of the cathedral, on the left, in the open air, I saw a large crucifix. In front of it was a light railing used to support passersby who kneel. Framed, for their use, was the text, in large letters, of the celebrated sonnet "To *Jesu Crucificado*", which is sometimes attributed to Saint Francis Xavier but is actually by an unknown author of an earlier period. This poetic masterpiece is the most magnificent expression of pure love. I have seen ordinary men and women reading the sonnet on their knees, remaining a moment in silence to pray. And what I afterward learned was that this sonnet figures not only in the anthologies of Christian texts but also in modern books of religious instruction in Spain.[5]

Those most attached to rituals are not necessarily those who have less soul.

Retraction

I wrote around 1938: "It is flattering oneself to believe that by denying the progress of one's own century one is insuring the heritage of all the treasures of former centuries." I still think that. But faced with what is now the reverse situation, I would write: "It is flattering oneself to believe that by denying the heritage of all former treasures one is insuring the progress of one's own century."

I also wrote: "If the spirit is lacking, dogma is no longer anything but a myth, and the Church is no longer anything but a faction." I still think so. But what has happened since then would prompt me today to write the complementary truth: "If dogma is

---

[5] The text is given as an appendix to this book.

lacking, the spirit is no longer anything but wind, and the Church becomes a progressivist faction."

I also wrote: "Before being a hope for the future, eternal life is a requirement for the present." I think that more than ever. But in an extroverted time, which no longer understands interiority, in order not to be misinterpreted, I would have to add: The requirement for eternal life in the present is the inner strength that lifts us out of the surface level of existence, prevents us from getting bogged down in the activity of the hour; it is the voice that commands us not to sacrifice the unique essence for the multifaceted current event.

I have been told: "Be modest, be humble; don't believe too strongly in your Christianity; yes, it is very fine, I will concede you that, but don't make an absolute of it. Don't forget that others, under other skies, have invented many other things to give a meaning to their life; your path is only one path among others; don't contrive privileges for yourself, don't claim an illusory monopoly. Be modest, be humble . . ."

This discourse would be excellent if "Christianity" were my fabrication—or that of my ancestors; if I congratulated myself for possessing it as my own property. But if I believe in Jesus Christ, such remarks cannot convince me. I can only understand them as follows:

"Be reasonable, don't lose yourself by giving yourself to Jesus Christ, don't commit yourself to him unconditionally; keep some room for falling back. Don't take his absolute claims in complete seriousness. He lacked humility, modesty: it is a common temptation among great 'spiritual men'. Those who followed him too closely lacked those qualities just as much: Francis of Assisi, Ignatius of Loyola, John of the Cross . . . They did not know how to express that impulse of negation and sacrifice that alone would have made them truly religious men. Their attention to the inner Spirit weakened, they gave in to the appeal of positive religion that makes things more secure. We need a new type of fully adult saint today. We need saints who know how to receive the divine Presence in themselves in the infinitely varied plurality of experiences instead of following Jesus alone. For close to twenty centuries, this element inspired by passion has favored narrowness, a possessive spirit, egotism, and pride. It is necessary at last to free ourselves from it."

Having heard this discourse, having understood well the sublimity of it, I gaze at my crucifix, and I ask Jesus to keep me faithful.

While all piety is so easily repudiated by scornfully calling it pietism, while all concern for morality is dismissed by the derogatory word moralism and all recognition of paternity is brushed aside by insisting on seeing only paternalism in it, why is so glorious a fate given to "pluralism"?

Everything that enriches unity is good; everything that goes against unity is bad; the plurality of convergence is good; the plurality of divergence (pluralism?) is bad.

The New Testament is full of appeals to unity, and to the closest and deepest unity. We would seek in vain there for the least appeal to "pluralism". We can find in the history of the Church numerous texts celebrating the variety of men, of their resources, of the different elements that are gathered together in Catholic unity; but it is always in order to admire that gathering together in that unity. We never find it celebrated for itself; unity, on the other hand, is admired and sought for itself.

⚜

The man of today, it has been written, must "sort out" the systems of values, ideologies, religions "that philosophical pluralism offers him every day". That is very much the current meaning of "pluralism", which consists of contradictory diversities. That is why it is not really advisable to use the word to designate the different possible expressions of the same Christian faith.

I am neither for unitarianism nor for pluralism but for plural unity or unified plurality.

Pluralism of integration, yes; pluralism of dissolution, no. —Pluralism on departure, in order to converge at the center; not pluralism on arrival, by distancing oneself from the center. —Diversity ordered to unity, and not diversification, shattered unity.

Nothing is more unproductive than difference cultivated for its own sake. Whatever the individual or the group, the search for originality is always inversion.

Seek first for the truth, and the new will perhaps be given you besides.

There is only a hair's breadth between the most profound faith and the most radical atheism—but this breadth is an abyss. The bridegroom recognizes his bride "by a single hair of her neck".

O "creativity"! How much destruction accomplished in your name!

Is tradition a weight that curbs spontaneity or the ground that supports it? The nourishing ground from which it draws its strength? Moreover, is it not that very strength without which all spontaneity dissipates and dies away? (Saint Basil).

It is a question of knowing if I want to be faithful to the authority of a living tradition in which and by which I live, or if I prefer to bind myself to the tyrannical caprices of opinion.

An absolute freedom is as if there were no ground under my steps; even more: as if the air outside stopped forcing its way into my lungs.

Absolute freedom is contrary to all rigorous thinking. In an atmosphere without resistance, thought dissipates, it evaporates or grows weak. Having too much ease, it becomes a game; having nothing to combat, it commits itself to nothing. A little constraint is not only inevitable but indispensable. In order to be vigorous, a thought must jump over an obstacle.

⚜

Never more than today has the mystery of the nuptial union between the "Lamb that was slain" and the "Bride of the Lamb" been lived. The Lamb was slain by "his own"—and it is by her own that the Church of today is united with him.

"One always believes that tradition is a thing of the past and that it is no more than a kind of object of historical awareness. One always supposes that it constitutes what is properly situated behind us, although we are, as it were, facing it—for it is our very destiny" (M. Heidegger, *Was heisst Denken?*, unpublished trans. M. de Diéguez).

"We confine ourselves", says this prelate, "to Vatican II, which is for us the authentic interpretation of the Gospel." Some great "Thomists" once spoke that way: With the *Summa*, they had the Gospel in hand, having finally arrived at its perfection. No more need of the evangelists or Paul or the Fathers; they even had to be avoided as dangerous; any doctor prior to Thomas smelled of heterodoxy. That was a betrayal of Saint Thomas; it is today a betrayal of Vatican II. And there is worse in store.

To escape the tradition of the Church, two opposing methods can be used for the same destructive result; either dispute everything that is not literally in the New Testament, in the same words; or say the Church has still not become fully aware of what she has a right to do and change. A third, more unscrupulous process combines the two preceding ones: by an ingenious "hermeneutics", make the sacred text say what one wishes to think and do today.

If there is nothing, or nearly nothing, new offered by Christianity; if it has not overturned the world, if for twenty centuries Christian holiness has been only a sterile illusion, then the myopia of our critics, who pull the Gospel to pieces, is supreme clairvoyance. But they would do well, in advance, to make sure of this.

To think of eternity is not to desert history; to esteem prayer and the interior life is not to neglect social life; to refuse to serve totalitarian atheism is not to become a henchman for reactionaries.

"Traditional Catholicism. . . ." So begins the Jaurès pamphlet that *L'Express* published in 1960. Already with these first words, what appears to be preciseness is, on the contrary, equivocation. "Traditional Catholicism" is in reality a pleonasm. Catholicism is traditional or it is not Catholicism. But by the choice of this adjective, which he inflates with a pejorative sense, the author lets us understand that it is not Catholicism itself that he wants to attack. Now it is, nevertheless, very much Catholicism itself, which is to say, Catholicism as a whole, that he is undertaking to attack. According to him, he would challenge only a certain way of professing Catholicism, characteristic of a certain milieu weighed down with its human traditions, and his generous language helps to maintain the illusion. But let one read it dispassionately and one soon perceives: his grudge is with the very substance of Catholicism; it is the whole Christian mystery that he rejects, it is faith in Jesus Christ itself that is his target.

The Modernists of 1907 and the Progressives of 1977: the former, deprived of the sacraments, experienced acute suffering; Alfred Loisy, the day the validity of his *celebret* [6] expired, was in distress. The latter cheerfully deprive themselves of the sacraments; they "liberate" themselves from them and give themselves as examples to a Church they want completely secularized.

[6] The ecclesiastical authority given to a priest to celebrate Mass.—TRANS.

It was during the Middle Ages, reputed to be a period marked by the supremacy of "clerics", that the councils made a large place for the laity: at the Lateran, at Lyons, at Vienne—well before Constance and Basel.

"[In May 1968] the fanatical objectification of knowledge about man suddenly appeared as a veritable Babylonian captivity, far from any spiritual connection. Intelligence was thought to be reduced to the sole analytical mechanism, that which makes of the world a machine because the understanding itself has chosen to be such. If a great denial is necessary, it is that of the claim of the understanding alone to know man thoroughly, and thus to remake him. Through the breach that must one day be opened in the positivist wall, whose defenders are still in place, and into the ranks of the theoreticians of denial, it is the universal fabric of values, the chief words held up to ridicule, their mystery, in which reason and heart commune, that will rush to enrich our arid mental space" (Pierre Emmanuel, *Discours de réception à l'Académie française*, June 6, 1969).

"Little sorcerers proliferate. It is a matter of who cries the loudest: 'I am liberated! Liberate yourselves!' It is enough to have abandoned publicly, in front of a crowd warned in advance, a few explicit dogmas, some 'principles' of conduct that were already less than clear, and above all some customs that were dying out on their own anyway. All that remains is to take up the collection. A fine feat!

"... The condition of prophet is assumed only by suffering beings, rolled despite themselves under the palm that kneads them and shapes them. To keep from speaking, they would flee all the way to Tarsus" (Gabriel Germain, *Le Regard intérieur* [Paris: Seuil, 1969], pp. 15, 34).

Karl Barth, on Schleiermacher:

"It is impossible to study Schleiermacher without being strongly impressed—and always in direct proportion to the degree one has penetrated his thought—by the richness and breadth of the tasks this man set himself, by the store of moral and intellectual knowledge he had at his disposal in undertaking them, by the virile perseverance with which he went to the very end of that to which he had committed himself, without being concerned to know if the circumstances were favorable for him or not, and by the skill he used for each of his works down to the Sunday sermon, as if he did it all effortlessly, and with such great reliability. . . .

"He was bound to Jesus by a personal relationship that is rightly characterized as love. . . . He was a straightforward man of the Church. Throughout his life, he thought, spoke, and acted in an awareness of his concrete responsibility" *(La Théologie protestante au XIXe siècle,* trans. L. Jeanneret [Geneva: Labor et Fides, 1969], pp. 234, 459; the work is from 1946).

That praise would apply equally as well to Hans Urs von Balthasar.

IV

The Rock of Faith

"Jesus founded neither the Church nor her institution. Biblically and historically, it is impossible to prove an act of foundation" (Gotthold Hasenhüttl, "Église et institution", *Concilium* 94 [1974]: 22).

Obviously. There is not much chance that this notarized act will be discovered in the caves of the Dead Sea or in the sands of the nearby desert, with the official signatures in due form.

⚜

Excerpts from Stanley L. Jaki, *And on This Rock: The Witness of One Land and Two Countries* (Notre Dame, Ind.: Ave Maria Press, 1978), chapter 3, "A Man Called Rock", pp. 71–90:

"In spite of having named and made Simon the Rock, Christ kept referring to him as Simon, son of Jonah. Such was Christ's subtle way of making it clear that as long as he was visibly present he alone was the spiritual Rock.... [Yet] while recalling long-past encounters between Christ and Simon, the Evangelists referred to Simon as Cephas, without forgetting that Christ addressed him as Simon" (p. 79).

"Jesus and the Twelve must have been impressed by the massive wall of rock rising over the source of the Jordan. Here was a sacred river taking its origin through an opening in a massive wall of rock, an opening which could evoke the wide-open jaws of death.... Against this backdrop Jesus spoke to Simon: 'You are Rock and on this rock I will build my church, and the jaws of death shall not prevail against it.'

"That such was the background will not appear a mere conjecture if one is ready to go by Matthew's instruction ... to 'the neighborhood of Caesarea Philippi' as that very background. It will appear even less of a conjecture if one recalls Jesus' fondness for choosing appropriate backdrops for his words [Jacob's well, the feast of Tabernacles, the ripening harvest, the little children]" (pp. 79–80).

"[Jesus] certainly knew that being called Rock (*sur*) was a most sacred privilege of Yahweh throughout the whole Old Testament.... He knew what was implied in his calling Simon, a mere man, *kepha* or Rock, a word closely synonymous with *sur*. He certainly knew how much more was implied in turning that mere man into the Rock on which he would build his church with a stability that was a sharing in the permanence of Yahweh himself" (p. 81).

"That a massive rock with a gaping cave in it was the background of Christ's words to Peter will forever remain beyond the reach of rigorous proof. What can be rigorously proven is the background voice of the Old Testament.... One would try in vain to find [that voice of the Old Testament] in learned books on Peter, written by biblical scholars [with the exception of Ridolfi, a Catholic priest, but not a biblical scholar, who alone gives a fairly explicit treatment of that voice in *Simon Pierre rocher biblique* (Paris: Apostolat des Éditions, 1965)]. Unless one keeps that voice in mind and unless one recalls its ultimate provenance, one shall never suspect the real meaning of the fact that through the Word of God there is a mere man called and made the Rock.

"And what a mere unreliable man he was! What a contrast.... Yet Simon's God-given name and Simon's God-decreed reality as Rock made sense only if they embodied somehow the characteristic of permanence in that very sense in which the Church was to be an enduring entity. Simon, the Rock, did not exist for himself but for the Church whose foundation he was to remain forever" (pp. 81–82) [See also chapter 2: "God the Rock", pp. 55–69.]

How humiliating it is—sad, disconcerting, tragic—to observe that, in fact, thoughts of eternity are what attach us most strongly to earth! What is it that makes me most love some men, makes me most grieve their disappearance, if not what was eternal in what they conceived, what they loved? But to attach oneself in that way to thoughts of the eternal, to attach oneself temporally, is there not a contradiction there? Is it not, actually, an impious negation, blasphemy? Is it not, in fact, to consider these thoughts as the finest inventions of man? It is to pretend, then, as if they were, without doubt, truly good things worthy of being loved, but, in the end, things of the earth.

But how would they appear to us otherwise? And as long as we are on earth, where could their charm come from if not from the wholly ephemeral and the wholly particular that colors them, just as from the very contrast that arises between the eternity of their content and the fragility of their form? As for that attachment we experience in their regard, does it not also necessarily stem from what we sense as perishable in us? So, what should be and what seemed at first to be, within time, a nostalgia for eternity, turns as if inevitably, with respect to eternity, into nostalgia for the time that eludes us. . . . Yet, to wish to admire, to savor in this way thoughts of eternity by taking them in their temporal particularity, insofar as they were prepared, lived, defended in some certain time and place, under some certain circumstances, with their tragic procession of incomprehension, battles, sufferings; to be attached in a spirit of ownership to what has authentic existence only through the negation of any ownership; to fall back as if on a thing of the past on something whose purpose is to pull us out of the slavery of the past: it is always the same illusion, and, left to ourselves, we are no more advanced than so many others before us; not only as to the will, of course, but also as to the spirit. The illusion is forever born in us; it is nourished by what should dissipate it; it corrupts the purest element of the spiritual life and transforms it into poison.

"All the cymbals of integrism will not extinguish the whisper of the Spirit" (Jules Monchanin, letter to Edouard Duperray, June 29, 1951).

Integrism has changed camp; its cymbals are only the more resounding. They think they are capable of making the walls of Jericho fall down, of winning over even the defenders of the Holy City. One could believe that the Church will be destroyed by them tomorrow...

But the whisper of the Spirit will not be extinguished. And like the light breeze that passes over Elijah, it bears the Life that will not be extinguished.

Discerning ideologues, or those who believe themselves so, assure us that doubt is an indispensable ingredient of faith: not only that there will always be a share of doubt in a believing conscience, but that doubt is included in the very idea of faith. They assure us that it is therefore important to maintain and cultivate doubt in oneself in the form of perpetual restlessness—and this does not refer to the restlessness of which Saint Augustine, Saint Anselm, or Saint

Thomas Aquinas spoke! Thus, by suggestion, they sow perplexity, defeatism, trouble, and a bad conscience in the souls of believers who listen to them, and then they congratulate themselves on their victory. They are, moreover, very confident themselves in their theory of doubt; it is for them an a priori principle that does not include the least particle of doubt as being, as they say, valid. They do not need reasons to doubt, any more than the pure fideist needs reasons to believe.

Saint Paul exhorted the faithful otherwise: "Beloved brothers, be steadfast, immovable.... Stand firm in your faith, be courageous, be strong" (1 Cor 15:58; 16:13). And Saint Peter, completing these orders: "Always be prepared to make a defense to any one who calls you to account for the hope that is in you" (1 Pet 3:15).

"I quite understand you: you are a good visionary for what is distant. But up close you get tired" (response of the corporal to Lieutenant Péguy, in *Réponse brève à Jaurès* [1900]; cf. *Œuvres en prose*, La Pléiade, vol. 1 [Paris: Gallimard, 1959], p. 279).

Many, on the contrary, are untiring up close and not only get tired of looking at the distant, of grasping a whole, of seeing it in a still larger whole—but they are blind to that; like the one who can look at a face only point by point, through a microscope.

⚜

I would be more intimidated by our critics, to whom every aspect of the Christian faith and the Church fall prey these days, if they themselves did not so often give me proof that they do not understand what they are criticizing and that in fact it is their critical bias that closes their eyes to it.

⚜

Up until the Constantinian period, "little emphasis was placed on hierarchy, authority and orthodoxy" (Donald Warwick, "The Centralization of Ecclesiastical Authority: An Organizational Perspective", *Concilium* 91 [January 1974]: 111):
  O Paul! O Clement! O Ignatius! O Irenaeus! . . .

⚜

"The institutional side of the Church is essentially a human product. . . . Now what man produced can necessarily be changed" (Gotthold Hasenhüttl, "Église et Institution", *Concilium* 91 [January 1974]: 22).
  Pour Twelve! Poor Peter!—Poor Jesus, poor Holy Spirit!

⚜

"In Antioch, something new dawned, through the impetus of a local clergyman."

That is how one writes the ancient history of the Church in the postconciliar era! And these lines are by an excellent bishop, wanting to teach his people. . . . Indeed, our bishops must follow the new experts they have acquiesced in accepting!

Nunc dimittis.—This *Nunc dimittis* every evening: how many times it is clouded with a melancholy that I have difficulty dissipating—that does not dissipate noticeably! What have my eyes seen during the day? The still-veiled coming of the Savior? Or his absence among us, or rather, his rejection? Again yesterday, among those who seemingly ought to be more closely attached to him, from one of them, this remark: "Jesus? For me, he was a man who was searching." And still worse remarks from others. But here, this evening, I had a visit from a true disciple of Jesus. Here was the discreet, penetrating, stimulating light—impossible to confuse with the mere radiance of a happy disposition. And here, once again, in all his mysterious force, the Savior reveals himself. He is there. "Viderunt oculi mei Salutare tuum [my eyes have seen your salvation]".

"The priest will be a man of faith and a messenger of faith only on condition that he is a man of prayer. If theology ceased to be a 'theology on one's knees' . . . , losing its way along paths of an intellectualism hypnotized by the problems thrown with almost sadistic insistence in the face of the Church, . . . it would no longer be a theology; it would become debased into a retarded 'bourgeois' dilletantism" (Karl Rahner, *Serviteurs du Christ*, trans. C. Muller [Tours: Mame, 1969], p. 126).

Occasionally "popular" Catholicism, scorned by a certain "elitism", is defended, and rightly so. But perhaps we should reject this kind of disjunction. Perhaps, too, it is not sufficiently noted (unless this is merely a polite silence?) that the "elitists" do not always constitute an elite, either from the point of view of intellectual culture or from a Christian point of view. Without wishing to intrude into anyone's conscience, one really cannot help seeing that these clerics who treat with scorn so many Catholics who are just "fulfilling obligations" scarcely give proof themselves of fidelity to the Church and the Gospel. It seems, on the other hand, that in their eyes one can be part of the "elite" only to the degree of his own "secularization". And yet I see almost everywhere an elite group of Christians, not numerous and not seeking to call themselves elite, strong in their faith, devoted to their neighbor, not advertising themselves, sometimes rich with human culture, to whom it would be ridiculous to apply the title "popular Catholicism", even without the scorn and irony. These would not dream of looking down on "popular Catholicism".

Our bishops, as well as numerous priests and laymen, have been intimidated, paralyzed, spellbound by the successive campaigns conducted under the reign of slogan words, equivocal banners: secularization, de-clergification, pluralism, orthopraxy, liberation, and so on.

Orthodoxy, orthopraxy: let us drop these abstract words, the second of which is brandished about by pedants, and the first of which is not justified by itself. Let us take the simple words of Scripture and tradition: faith, charity. And let us recognize that it is illusory to imagine that we will guard the second by dismissing the first, just as it is illusory to imagine that we will guard the first if we refuse to make it bear its fruits through the second. History shows this clearly enough. The present reality, unfortunately, confirms it.

There is no *Evangelium Christi* once the *Evangelium de Christo* is dissolved. Post-Christianity becomes a neo-paganism, worse than the old one. The "perfume of an empty vase" is soon dissipated, and the vase receives an entirely different content.

From a catechetical program (May 1974): "Transmission of Faith: NO.—Engendering to Life: YES." A fine example of dichotomy. Is there no life of faith? Is true faith not a life? The catechumen comes to ask for "faith"; he is taught the Creed, and the bishop baptizes him: he is thus engendered to the life of faith.

Ideologues had started by dismissing religion in the name of faith; now we have them dismissing faith in the name of life. Tomorrow, it will be even clearer: they will dismiss life (that divine life received by grace that comes from the Gospel) in the name of some political membership.

A group of neo-Christians teach us that "prayer must no longer be addressed to God the Creator but to God the father of all men." Admirable dichotomy! I prefer to continue to say, with our old Apostles' Creed: "I believe in God the Father Almighty, *creator* of heaven and earth."

Another group has decided, it says, to "reject the traditional expression of faith, which is tied to the prevailing ideology", in order to invent another one. In other words, they reject the traditional faith, which has remained the same for nearly twenty centuries—through a hundred different ideologies with which it has never been aligned—in order to adopt a new "expression", tied to some ideology in favor today.

Still another group wants to change the order of the Creed by inverting the trinitarian formula. Up until today, no one had thought it absurd to begin with the Father and to pass through the Son in order finally to reach the Spirit, present in the heart of the community. They posed the "most obscure" first, closing their eyes to "what one could see in everyday life and in a certain number of signs, like the sacraments".

Let us salute these new Christians, who see the Holy Spirit directly and clearly when they are present at a baptism or a confirmation. But they then tell us that what they advocate is a return to a certain human experience, the "center, source, and foundation" of everything. The revelation of the Father by the Son (including the action of the Spirit) is in their eyes nothing but an ideology that has become "foreign" to them . . .

Nothing is easier for a "psychologist", whether psychoanalyst or not and of whatever persuasion, than to caricature everything about Christian life, and most particularly Catholic life, whether familial, monastic, or apostolic, whether that of yesterday, long ago, or today. He will always have an audience, filled with admiration for his scientific jargon, proud to participate through his mediation in the "conquests of science". He will be able to do the same for the Gospel, and if he is legion, like the famous demon, and if he finds himself supported, moreover, by some of those anti-Christian fanatics of whom no generation is deprived, he will be able to ruin the contribution of the Gospel in a whole society.

But he will never have understood a thing about it.

Those who oppose their "personal experience" to the norms of the tradition, dogma, discipline, and liturgy of the Church: with what poor banalities, sentimentality, platitudes, slogans, and ephemeral fantasies they will end up! And if, being clerics, they abuse the trust they hold from the Church in order to impose them on others, is there any lower tyranny?

Newman did not set his "experience" in opposition to the "ideology" of dogma! With what emphasis he sang the praises of the most "objective", the most apparently abstract, the most impersonal of all the normative texts of the faith, the Creed attributed to Saint Athanasius (cf. *Grammar of Assent* [Notre Dame and London: Univ. of Notre Dame Press, 1979], pp. 122–23). What unenthusiastic mistrust he would arouse in our new prophets and our new mystics!

Those who really want to accommodate some particular truth of the faith because it corresponds, they say, to their own experience either reduce it to nothing and, isolating it, distort it, or else they forget that it is this truth that has already shaped their experience—and in either case, they foolishly set themselves up as the supreme criterion.

If only they would let their experience be expanded and deepened by the submission of their spirit to the total mystery: that is the only logical attitude of faith.

These pseudo-theologians who call themselves "critics", carrying on to their heart's content the "critical function" of theology and destroying the rocks of the Church one by one—it is so obvious that they no longer understand anything about it: they have put themselves outside—and that is infinitely worse (because it is exactly the opposite) than still being outside.

"Ever since there ceased to be a Pope-King, the divested papacy, having become in a more striking way the ideal and immaterial center, the inviolable Rome of the great Catholic empire—the only inviolable Rome since it is the intangible Rome—seems to sense that in the desperate eagerness of nations and classes, humanity is waiting for an arbiter" (James Darmesteter, *Les Prophètes d'Israël* [Paris: Lévy, 1892], pp. xviii–xix).

⚜

What one dares not say, what one neither can nor wants to say, what one scarcely dares think in a fleeting way, what one immediately strives to forget, but what is nevertheless the real truth, the certain historical reality: all the very diverse Protestant ecclesiologies are of human creation, invented according to circumstances, in order to justify and to make viable de facto situations. The great "Reformers", who had not in the least dreamed at first of breaking with the one Church, but precisely to reform her, were then led despite themselves to organize in a visible way those who had followed them in their split, each of them according to a different type. It was then necessary to rework the history of Christian origins according to these types. And the whole effort of "criticism" was exercised for this purpose.

There was enough of the "accidental" accumulated in the course of the centuries, both good and bad, in any case contingent, to provide food for this criticism and, in places where it proceeded from a questionable a priori, a provisional appearance of reason.

Yet, "I wonder", writes J. J. Allman, "if, once the division of the Christian West became set, the profound reason why this tradition [of the 'Catholic' structure of the primitive Church] is challenged ... does not come from a wish, whether conscious or unconscious, ... to justify a multiplicity of ecclesial structures with, as a corollary, the right to settle down in Christian division with a clear conscience" (in *Les Sacrements d'initiation et les ministères sacrés* [Paris: Fayard, 1974], p. 239).

Just as euthanasia is an assassination, or a suicide, secularization, such as it is advocated and the process of it applied, is an apostasy. Hypocritical language for a hypocritical operation. But the essential reality is the same. There is no need to cover it with deceptive words.

Appendix

To *Jesu Crucificado*

O God, I love thee, I love thee—
Not out of hope of heaven for me
Nor fearing not to love and be
    In the everlasting burning.
Thou, thou, my Jesus, after me
    Didst reach thine arms out dying,
For my sake sufferedst nails and lance,
Mocked and marrèd countenance,
    Sorrows passing number,
    Sweat and care and cumber,
Yea and death, and this for me,
    And thou couldst see me sinning:
Then I, why should not I love thee,
Jesu, so much in love with me?
Not for heaven's sake; not to be
Out of hell by loving thee;
Not for any gains I see;
But just the way that thou didst me
I do love and I will love thee:
What must I love thee, Lord, for then?
For being my king and God. Amen.

This prayer is also known under the title of the first verse: "O Deus, ego amo Te". [The translation here is by Gerard Manley Hopkins, S.J.]